AMERICAN LEGAL SYSTEMS:
A RESOURCE AND REFERENCE GUIDE

ANDERSON'S
Law School Publications

Administrative Law Anthology
Thomas O. Sargentich

Administrative Law: Cases and Materials
Daniel J. Gifford

An Admiralty Law Anthology
Robert M. Jarvis

Alternative Dispute Resolution: Strategies for Law and Business
E. Wendy Trachte-Huber and Stephen K. Huber

American Legal Systems: A Resource and Reference Guide
Toni M. Fine

Analytic Jurisprudence Anthology
Anthony D'Amato

An Antitrust Anthology
Andrew I. Gavil

Appellate Advocacy: Principles and Practice, Third Edition
Ursula Bentele and Eve Cary

Basic Accounting Principles for Lawyers: With Present Value and Expected Value
C. Steven Bradford and Gary A. Ames

A Capital Punishment Anthology (with Electronic Caselaw Appendix)
Victor L. Streib

Cases and Problems in Criminal Law, Third Edition
Myron Moskovitz

The Citation Workbook: How to Beat the Citation Blues, Second Edition
Maria L. Ciampi, Rivka Widerman, and Vicki Lutz

Civil Procedure Anthology
David I. Levine, Donald L. Doernberg, and Melissa L. Nelken

Civil Procedure: Cases, Materials, and Questions, Second Edition
Richard D. Freer and Wendy Collins Perdue

Federal Rules of Civil Procedure, 1998-99 Edition
Publisher's Staff

Clinical Anthology: Readings for Live-Client Clinics
Alex J. Hurder, Frank S. Bloch, Susan L. Brooks, and Susan L. Kay

Commercial Transactions Series: Problems and Materials
Louis F. Del Duca, Egon Guttman, Alphonse M. Squillante, Fred H. Miller, Linda Rusch, and
Peter Winship
    Vol. 1: Secured Transactions Under the UCC
    Vol. 2: Sales Under the UCC and the CISG
    Vol. 3: Negotiable Instruments Under the UCC and the CIBN

Communications Law: Media, Entertainment, and Regulation
Donald E. Lively, Allen S. Hammond, Blake D. Morant, and Russell L. Weaver

A Conflict-of-Laws Anthology
Gene R. Shreve

Constitutional Conflicts
Derrick A. Bell, Jr.

A Constitutional Law Anthology, Second Edition
Michael J. Glennon, Donald E. Lively, Phoebe A. Haddon, Dorothy E. Roberts,
    and Russell L. Weaver

Constitutional Law: Cases, History, and Dialogues
Donald E. Lively, Phoebe A. Haddon, Dorothy E. Roberts, and Russell L. Weaver

The Constitutional Law of the European Union
James D. Dinnage and John F. Murphy

The Constitutional Law of the European Union: Documentary Supplement
James D. Dinnage and John F. Murphy

Constitutional Torts
Sheldon H. Nahmod, Michael L. Wells, and Thomas A. Eaton

Contract Law and Practice
Gerald E. Berendt, Michael L. Closen, Doris Estelle Long, Marie A. Monahan, Robert J. Nye,
    and John H. Scheid

A Contracts Anthology, Second Edition
Peter Linzer

Contracts: Contemporary Cases, Comments, and Problems
Michael L. Closen, Richard M. Perlmutter, and Jeffrey D. Wittenberg

A Copyright Anthology: The Technology Frontier
Richard H. Chused

Corporate Law Anthology
Franklin A. Gevurtz

Corporate and White Collar Crime: An Anthology
Leonard Orland

A Criminal Law Anthology
Arnold H. Loewy

Criminal Law: Cases and Materials
Arnold H. Loewy

A Criminal Procedure Anthology
Silas J. Wasserstrom and Christie L. Snyder

Criminal Procedure: Arrest and Investigation
Arnold H. Loewy and Arthur B. LaFrance

Criminal Procedure: Trial and Sentencing
Arthur B. LaFrance and Arnold H. Loewy

Economic Regulation: Cases and Materials
Richard J. Pierce, Jr.

Elements of Law
Eva H. Hanks, Michael E. Herz, and Steven S. Nemerson

Ending It: Dispute Resolution in America
    Descriptions, Examples, Cases and Questions
Susan M. Leeson and Bryan M. Johnston

An Environmental Law Anthology
Robert L. Fischman, Maxine I. Lipeles, and Mark S. Squillace

Environmental Law Series
Jackson B. Battle, Robert L. Fischman, Maxine I. Lipeles, and Mark S. Squillace
    Vol. 1: Environmental Decisionmaking: NEPA and the Endangered Species Act,
        Second Edition
    Vol. 2: Water Pollution, Second Edition
    Vol. 3: Air Pollution, Second Edition
    Vol. 4: Hazardous Waste, Third Edition

Environmental Protection and Justice
  Readings and Commentary on Environmental Law and Practice
Kenneth A. Manaster

European Union Law Anthology
Karen V. Kole and Anthony D'Amato

An Evidence Anthology
Edward J. Imwinkelried and Glen Weissenberger

Federal Antitrust Law: Cases and Materials
Daniel J. Gifford and Leo J. Raskind

Federal Evidence Courtroom Manual
Glen Weissenberger

Federal Income Tax Anthology
Paul L. Caron, Karen C. Burke, and Grayson M.P. McCouch

Federal Rules of Evidence Rules, Legislative History, Commentary and Authority
  1998-99 Edition
Glen Weissenberger

Federal Rules of Evidence Handbook, 1998-99 Edition
Publisher's Staff

Federal Wealth Transfer Tax Anthology
Paul L. Caron, Grayson M.P. McCouch, Karen C. Burke

First Amendment Anthology
Donald E. Lively, Dorothy E. Roberts, and Russell L. Weaver

International Environmental Law Anthology
Anthony D'Amato and Kirsten Engel

International Human Rights: Law, Policy, and Process, Second Edition
Frank C. Newman and David Weissbrodt

Selected International Human Rights Instruments and
  Bibliography For Research on International Human Rights Law, Second Edition
Frank C. Newman and David Weissbrodt

International Intellectual Property Anthology
Anthony D'Amato and Doris Estelle Long

International Law Anthology
Anthony D'Amato

International Law Coursebook
Anthony D'Amato

Introduction to the Study of Law: Cases and Materials
John Makdisi

Judicial Externships: The Clinic Inside the Courthouse
Rebecca A. Cochran

A Land Use Anthology
Jon W. Bruce

AMERICAN LEGAL SYSTEMS:
A RESOURCE AND REFERENCE GUIDE

TONI M. FINE

NEW YORK UNIVERSITY
SCHOOL OF LAW

ANDERSON PUBLISHING CO.
CINCINNATI

AMERICAN LEGAL SYSTEMS: A RESOURCE AND REFERENCE GUIDE
TONI M. FINE

© 1997 by Anderson Publishing Co.

Second Printing — July, 1997
Third Printing — June, 1998
Fourth Printing — July, 1999

Anderson Publishing Co.
2035 Reading Road / Cincinnati, Ohio 45202
800-582-7295 / e-mail andpubco@aol.com / Fax 513-562-5430
World Wide Web http://www.andersonpublishing.com

ISBN: 0-87084-266-8

CONTENTS

PREFACE

It is my hope that *American Legal Systems: A Resource and Reference Guide* will be a unique addition to the abundance of literature designed to introduce students of many disciplines to the field of law. While books on legal research, legal writing, and jurisprudence abound, there is none that presents the fundamentals of the American legal systems in a comprehensive yet accessible way.

That is what *American Legal Systems* strives to do. The book provides an overview of American legal institutions and sources of law, and presents a guide to the interrelationships between and among those institutions and legal authorities. It discusses the defining role of the doctrine of *stare decisis* in the American common law system and the critical judicial review function. In addition, *American Legal Systems* shows the reader how to determine and apply the relative priorities of sources of law, all in the context of the legislative process, agency action, and principles of constitutional and legislative supremacy.

American Legal Systems ties many of these concepts to the realities of law practice. Portions of the book demonstrate how to locate specific resources, use legal terms, and prepare commonplace legal documents.

Among the main virtues of the book is its "reader-friendliness." It introduces readers to some extremely complicated issues of American jurisprudence in a clear and straightforward way. It is relatively short and concise. Much of it is in chart form with supporting narrative, allowing the user to quickly find and assimilate sought-after information. *American Legal Systems* also contains a comprehensive index and extensive internal cross-references, enabling the reader to locate with great ease any term or concept used in the book. As such, *American Legal Systems* could be used for reference purposes in conjunction with a student's substantive course work, or it could be used in connection with an experiential task, such as legal research and writing.

Given my education and professional experience, I originally conceived *American Legal Systems* for law students, but I hope that it will also prove to be a valuable resource for members of the general public and for students of diverse disciplines: government, political science, pre-law studies, paralegal courses, and other areas of instruction. My hope is that *any* student of one or more of these areas will benefit from the foundation in the law presented in this book. While the paradigmatic audience for *American Legal Systems* remains students of law, it should be widely applicable to students in related disciplines.

Any comments on this first edition would be warmly received and much appreciated.

Toni M. Fine
New York City
1997

ACKNOWLEDGMENTS

I would like to thank the following for their useful comments on various drafts of this book: Carol Alpert, Rebekah Diller, Michael R. Glaser, Otto A. Haberstock, John F. Hirschman, Richard H. Levenson, Laura Moore, Andrea McArdle, and Nancy L. Schultz.

I also thank the hundreds of students over the years who have given voice to this book and whose relentless quest to learn and accomplish has inspired this work.

Finally, I thank Barbara J. Cohen for her invaluable assistance and for providing an atmosphere of composure during the final stages of this book.

A NOTE TO USERS OF
AMERICAN LEGAL SYSTEMS: A RESOURCE AND REFERENCE GUIDE

Two points bear special mention in connection with use of this book: First, *American Legal Systems* deals largely with matters of federal law. The laws of the various states are, of course, of critical importance to the practice of law. While this book has endeavored to explain state legal systems and to provide the reader with the necessary foundations of state law, a more comprehensive treatment was not feasible given the differences in laws and litigation and other procedures among the various states. Thus, the focus of much of this book is federal law, given both its own importance and its utility as a paradigm for the operation of many state systems. As often as is practicable, references to state law are included.

Second, there is little mention of computer-assisted legal research methods, despite their growing use and popularity. Most important in this decision is the recognition that a student must *first* master the fundamentals of the law and learn to use and appreciate the value of traditional research methods before computerized databases can be used effectively. Of secondary importance is that many students and practitioners do not have extensive access to computer databases. Finally, the most commonly-used legal research services offer manuals for use of their respective programs, which provide a more comprehensive presentation than could possibly be done here.

I hope that these omissions add to rather than detract from the utility of *American Legal Systems.*

CHAPTER I

BASIC CONCEPTS OF AMERICAN JURISPRUDENCE

A. Summary of Basic American Legal Principles

What follows are some of the fundamental principles that comprise the American legal system. Each of these is discussed in greater detail in this and other chapters of this book. They are summarized below in order to give the reader an overview of some of the basics of American common law.

1. Impact of Precedent—The Principle of *Stare Decisis*

The defining principle of common law[1] is the requirement that courts follow decisions of higher level courts within the same jurisdiction. It is from this legacy of *stare decisis* that a somewhat predictable, consistent body of law has emerged. See Chapters I.F. and II.G.

2. Court Hierarchy

Court level or hierarchy defines to a great degree the extent to which a decision by one court will have a binding effect on another court. The federal court system, for instance, is based on a three-tiered structure, in which the United States District Courts are the trial-level courts; the United States Court of Appeals is the first level court of appeal; and the United States Supreme Court is the final arbiter of the law. See Chapters I.F., I.G., I.H., II.G.1.

3. Jurisdiction

The term "jurisdiction" has two important meanings in American law. One meaning of "jurisdiction" refers to the formal power of a court to exercise judicial authority over a particular matter. Although the term most often is used in connection with the jurisdiction of a court over particular matters, one may also speak of matters being within or beyond the jurisdiction of any other governmental entity. See Chapters I.C.2., I.F., and I.H.1., 2., and 3.

---

[1] See Chapter I.B. for a discussion of the term "common law."

Second, the federal court system is based on a system of "jurisdictions," the geographic distribution of courts of particular levels. For instance, while there is only one Supreme Court, the court of appeals is divided into 13 circuits, and there are 94 district courts. See Chapter I.H.3. In addition, each state court system comprises its own "jurisdiction." As indicated above, the jurisdiction in which a case arose will determine which courts' decisions will be binding precedents. See Chapter I.F.

4. Mandatory/Binding versus Persuasive Authority

Some of the various sources of law that will be examined are considered to be "mandatory" or "binding," while other sources are considered to be merely "persuasive." See Chapter I.G. Indeed, a court may completely disregard precedent that is not binding (*i.e.*, not even consider it to be persuasive). The issue of whether authority is mandatory or persuasive relates directly to the application of *stare decisis* principles. See Chapter I.F.3.

5. Primary versus Secondary Authority

The various sources of law may also be broken down into primary and secondary sources of law. Primary sources of law may be mandatory on a particular court, or they may be merely persuasive. Whether they are binding or persuasive will depend on various factors.

Secondary authority is not itself law, and is *never* mandatory authority. A court may, however, look towards secondary sources of law for guidance as to how to resolve a particular issue. See Chapters I.G., II.B. Secondary authority is also useful as a case finding tool and for general information about a particular issue. See Chapters I.E., 1b. and 2.

6. Dual Court Systems

The American legal system is based on a system of federalism, or decentralization. While the national or "federal" government itself possesses significant powers, the individual states retain powers not specifically enumerated as exclusively federal. Most states have court systems which mirror that of the federal court system. See Chapter I.H.

7. Interrelationship Among Various Sources of Law

One of the more complex notions of American jurisprudence is the extent to which the various sources of law, from both the state and federal systems, interrelate with one another. There is a complex set of rules that defines the relative priority among various sources of law and between the state and federal systems. See Chapters I.H. and I.

B.   What Is Common Law?

The term "common law" evokes confusion and uncertainty—which is no surprise given its duality of meaning. The term "common law" may refer to any of the following:

1.   Common Law as Differentiated from Civil Law

The American system is a "common law" system, which relies heavily on court precedent in formal adjudications. In our common law system, even when a statute is at issue, judicial determinations in earlier court cases are extremely critical to the court's resolution of the matter before it. See Chapter I.I.3.

Civil law systems[2] rely less on court precedent and more on codes, which explicitly provide rules of decision for many specific disputes. When a judge needs to go beyond the letter of a code in disposing of a dispute, the judge's resolution will not become binding or perhaps even relevant in subsequent determinations involving other parties.

2.   Case Law

Common law may refer to "judge-made" law, otherwise known as case law. Cases are legal determinations based on a set of particular facts involving parties with a genuine interest in the controversy.

a.   Case Law May Be of Several General Types:

(1) *Pure decisional case law*—Court called upon to decide cases on the basis of prior court decisions (precedent) and/or policy and a sense of inherent fairness. In cases of pure decisional law, there is no applicable statute or constitutional provision that applies. This type of decisional law is what is referred to as "judicially-created doctrine." Historically, the term "case law" referred to certain areas of law (*e.g.,* torts, property) that began as judge-made, or pure decisional law.

(2) *Case law based on constitutional provisions*—Court called upon to consider whether a particular statute or governmental action is consistent with the United States Constitution or a particular state constitution. Court interpretation may rely upon prior decisional law interpreting same or some other constitutional provision.

---

[2]   Civil law systems are found in many European, Eastern, and Latin American countries, as well as in Louisiana.

    (3) *Case law based on statutory provisions*—Court called upon to interpret a statute. Court interpretation may rely upon prior decisional law interpreting the same or similar statute.

b. Subsequent Case History (see Chapter II.B.5):

    (1) Subsequent Case History defined—What a higher level court has done with respect to a lower-level court decision on appeal.

    (2) Importance of Subsequent Case History—If a higher level court has taken action on a lower level case, it is the opinion and holding of the *higher* level court that will constitute the precedent in the case. A higher level court opinion will in effect abrogate the lower level court opinion in the same case.

c. Subsequent Case Treatment (see Chapter II.B.5):

    (1) Subsequent Case Treatment defined—What other cases have said about the initial case. Has it been followed? Reversed? Distinguished? Applied in a specific way?

    (2) Importance of Subsequent Case Treatment—Will indicate how the same and other courts interpret the initial case.

C. The American Judicial System: A System Based on Advocacy and the Presence of Actual Controversy

    The American legal system is adversarial and is based on the premise that a real, live dispute involving parties with a genuine interest in its outcome will allow for the most vigorous legal debate of the issues, and that courts should not have the power to issue decisions unless they are in response to a genuine controversy. Hence, federal courts are prohibited from issuing "advisory" opinions, or opinions that do not involve a live case or controversy.[3]

1. Threshold Issues Designed to Preclude Advisory Opinions

    Given the prohibition against advisory opinions by the federal courts, there are certain threshold prerequisites which must be satisfied before a federal court will hear a case. Issues surrounding the applicability of these

---

[3] These principles are based on Article III of the U.S. Constitution, which limits federal court jurisdiction to "cases and controversies."

    Unlike the federal courts, some state *do* allow for the presentation of cases that are not based on live controversies, and hence do not share the federal court bias against advisory opinions.

prerequisites may also arise in state courts and on petitions for review of agency orders. See Chapter VI.C.1.

The principal prerequisites to court review are the following:

Standing—The parties must have an actual, cognizable, usually pecuniary or proprietary, interest in the litigation.

Finality—In the case of appeals or agency review, the action by the trial court or administrative body must be final and have a real impact on the parties.

Exhaustion—The parties must have exhausted any possible avenues for relief available in the trial court or administrative body.

Ripeness—The dispute must present a current controversy which has immediate rather than anticipated or hypothetical effects on the parties.

Mootness—The dispute must not have been resolved. Nor must the circumstances have changed in any way that renders the dispute no longer subject to controversy.

No Political Questions—Courts will not involve themselves in non-justiciable disputes that are between the other two branches of the federal government and are of a political nature.

While these prerequisites are well-established, the courts tend to apply them in a pragmatic way and allow exceptions to these requirements when warranted by the facts.

2. Courts Generally Confine Themselves to the Dispute Presented for Resolution

As a jurisdictional matter, courts are supposed to restrict their holdings to the narrowest terms possible in resolving a dispute.

This limitation relates to the principle of *dictum,* under which portions of the opinion not required for the resolution of the precise issues before the court on the facts presented by the parties are of diminished precedential value. See Chapter II.C.

3. Tendency to Avoid Constitutional Issues When Possible

Federal courts also tend to avoid deciding constitutional issues when they are able to decide a case on a procedural, statutory, or some other ground.

D. Institutional Roles in the American Legal System

1. Attorney

Depending upon the circumstances and the needs of the client, the lawyer may be a counselor, a negotiator, and/or a litigator. In each of these roles, the lawyer will need to engage in factual investigation.

With respect to each of these roles, the lawyer will do the following:

Counselor: Attorney will help advise the client how to order the client's affairs, how or whether to proceed with a proposed course of action, or how to proceed with respect to pending or potential litigation or settlement. Often, this is when the lawyer will prepare (or ask that someone prepare) an interoffice memorandum of law (see Chapter X.), which will examine the client's legal position and help the lawyer counsel the client.

Negotiator: Lawyer will work with opposing counsel to try to get a favorable resolution for the client with respect to a pending dispute. The parties may already be in litigation when they negotiate, or the parties, through their attorneys, may be negotiating a resolution to a dispute not yet in court. The art of negotiation involves many techniques individual to particular attorneys and the circumstances. The client always retains the right to accept or reject a settlement negotiated or offered by the opposing party.

Litigator: In litigating, the attorney will help pick a jury and participate in pre-trial motions. At trial, the attorney will present evidence through testimony of witnesses, documents and perhaps demonstrative evidence (*e.g.,* charts, diagrams). The lawyer will also present an opening statement and closing argument, and will make and respond to evidentiary objections lodged by the opposing party. The lawyer may also make motions, sometimes supported by a memorandum in support thereof (see Chapter XI) before the court, and propose to the court a set of jury instructions. See Chapter V.B.

Fact Investigator: All of the lawyer's roles require the investigation of relevant facts, including locating and interviewing witnesses.

A lawyer is to be a zealous advocate of his/her client. In this respect, the lawyer must advocate on the client's behalf and avoid conflicts of interest. The lawyer is also an officer of the court and is required to deal fairly and honestly with the court and with its other officers, including the lawyer's opponents.

There are specific ethical rules applicable to these issues, but in most circumstances, when the client's interests and those of the lawyer as officer of the court conflict or otherwise interfere with each other, the lawyer is generally expected to favor his or her role as advocate of the client.[4]

2. Judge

The judge is the final arbiter of the law. The judge is charged with the duty to state, as a positive matter, what the law is.

At trial, the judge takes a passive, "umpire" role in connection with the presentation of evidence by counsel. The judge must also make evidentiary rulings, and charge the jury as to the law to be applied. In addition, the judge is to maintain order in the courtroom.

Occasionally, when the parties agree, the judge may also act as trier of fact. This is known as a "bench trial." See Chapter V.B.

Judges in federal courts are appointed by the President with the "advice and consent" of the Senate. Many state court judges are elected by popular vote.

3. Jury

The jury, a group of local citizens, is the fact-finder in most trials. The jury will receive instructions from the judge as to the law, and its members will assess the facts as they perceive them in light of the law as instructed, to return a verdict. See Chapter V.B.

E.   Sources of Law

1. Overview of Primary and Secondary Authority

There are many sources which comprise "the law" in the United States. At least two major divisions between sources of law may be identified. First, there are primary and secondary sources of law, which are identified and discussed immediately below and in Chapter I.E.2., respectively.

Second, there are both federal and state sources of law. State sources of primary authority are addressed together with the primary sources of

---

[4]   Most states have adopted some variant of either the American Bar Association (ABA) Model Rules of Professional Conduct or the ABA Model Code of Professional Responsibility. The federal bar as well as many professional bar associations have also adopted standards based on these rules. There is also a special code of conduct applicable to government attorneys.

In addition, Rule 11 of the Federal Rules of Civil Procedure requires that a lawyer have a reasonable basis for believing the allegations set forth in all writings submitted to the court. See Chapter V.B.

federal law, below. Some secondary authorities are state-specific, or have sets that relate specifically to state law. See Chapter I.E.2.

a. Primary Sources of Law   Primary authority as a body constitutes "the law," the set of enforceable legal rules and principles. The following are the most significant sources of primary authority:[5]

(1) Constitutions

Constitutions are government charters. They provide the fundamental rights and obligations of citizens within the charter, and establish and ordain government systems.

U.S. Constitution: The document that establishes the federal government of the United States. No state or federal law can contravene any provision of the U.S. Constitution.

The U.S. Constitution establishes three branches of federal government:

    (a)   Legislative—2 houses (Congress = Senate + House of Representatives) with power to make laws.

    (b)   Executive—President and others to carry out laws.

    (c)   Judiciary—Supreme Court; Congress given authority to establish other federal courts.

State constitutions: Each state also has its own constitution. While a state constitution may confer rights greater than those conferred by the U.S. Constitution, it may not purport to limit or take away rights conferred by the U.S. Constitution or by federal statutes.

(2) Statutes

Federal: Laws passed by a majority vote of each house of Congress and then signed by the President. A presidential veto may be overriden, and in limited other situations, a bill can become law without presidential approval. See Chapters III.C. and D.

State: Each state may pass legislation according to rules applicable in that state.

No state law may contravene any provision of federal statutory or constitutional law.

State action may be preempted in certain areas when federal law so requires.

(3) Rules, Regulations, and Orders

---

[5] Treaties—international agreements—are also a form of primary authority. In some cases, treaties are self-executing. In other cases, they must be given effect by implementing legislation.

Federal: Federal agencies issue rules and regulations, and adjudicate, pursuant to statutory authority. See Chapters IV.A. and B.
States: States also have administrative agencies, which act pursuant to state legislative authority.
No action by any state agency may contravene any federal law nor may it deal with any matter preempted by federal law.

(4) Executive Orders and Proclamations
U.S. Presidential issuances. See Chapter IV.E. Presidential orders cannot legislate or reverse an act of Congress.
State governors may also issue orders and proclamations.

(5) Case Law/Common Law
Judge-made law/legal doctrine.
Case law is issued by federal and state courts.

b. Secondary Sources of Law   Secondary sources of law are not themselves law, but comment upon, analyze, discuss, interpret, and/or criticize primary authority. See Chapter I.E.2.

Examples of secondary authority are the following:
Treatises
Restatements
Law Reviews
American Law Reports (ALR)
Hornbooks
Legal Encyclopedias

State law may be discussed in any of the foregoing secondary authorities. Some states have their own legal encyclopedias.

c. Nature of Primary Versus Secondary Authority As Precedent
Primary authority may be mandatory *or* persuasive. Secondary authority may be persuasive, but is *never* mandatory. See Chapters I.A., F. and G.

2. Secondary Sources of Law

Secondary sources are not law, but they comment upon, summarize, restate, criticize, or advocate changes to the law.*

---

* Some secondary sources, such as case digests (see Chapter II.B.1), Shepard's Citators (see Chapter II.B.2.) and annotated versions of the United States Code (see Chapter III.B.) are case finding tools and do not share the functions of the secondary sources described herein. Unlike the secondary authorities discussed here, case finding tools may not be cited or quoted.

Among the purposes they serve are as case-finding tools (they cite to cases[6]), and as background information on an area of law.

Because secondary authorities are not themselves law, they are *never* binding authority. Depending upon the authority, they may be more or less persuasive, as indicated below.

Common sources of secondary authority are treatises, hornbooks, restatements, legal encyclopedias, law reviews, American Law Reports, Uniform and Model Acts, commercial looseleaf services, and litigation manuals.

a. Treatises

General Description/Overview	Specific treatment of multitude of issues in a particular area of law.
Special Features	Multi-volume; detailed; updated frequently.
Usefulness	Provides detailed information about a particular area of law.
Credibility As Authority	Certain writers considered to be most well-known authorities in a particular area. Some carry significant prestige with courts.

b. Hornbooks

General Description/Overview	Very general, background information.
Special Features	Not comprehensive; very concise and clear.
Usefulness	Useful if you have no familiarity at all with a topic.
Credibility As Authority	Generally do not carry much weight.

c. Legal Encyclopedias

General Description/Overview	Am. Jur. (American Jurisprudence) and C.J.S. (Corpus Jurus Secundum). Organized topically by legal issue, subject. Gives overview and guides user to primary authority and other resources.
Special Features	Am. Jur. has some state versions in addition to the national version.

---

6   The citations provided in secondary authorities are often *not* consistent with the *Bluebook*. See Chapter IX.

Usefulness	Case-finding tool—Leads to cases in many jurisdictions. Background; good place to begin when you know little or nothing about the subject.
Credibility As Authority	Very little authoritative value—do not cite except for most basic, well-accepted propositions (even then, only if necessary).

d. Restatements

General Description/Overview	State and analyze common law on national basis; show trends, make recommendations.
Special Features	Joint effort by scholars, judges, practitioners; panels of noted specialists in area. State general principles and give comments thereto.
Usefulness	Deal with various substantive topics, focusing on overview of state approaches. Appendix volumes contain case digests and citations.
Credibility As Authority	Excellent analyses, given considerable respect by courts, often adopted as law of state. Respectable to cite as secondary authority.

e. Law Reviews

General Description/Overview	Scholarly writings on discrete, fairly specific areas of law.
Special Features	Journals are usually student edited and operated. Journals are general or specific (by theme/area of law).
Usefulness	General scholarly interest.
Credibility as Authority	Not usually used or cited by practitioners. Nor will a court often consider a law review article to have persuasive value.

f. American Law Reports (A.L.R)

General Description/ Overview	Two components: • Cases—Limited number of cases "reported" [Note: never use the ALR "citation"]; • Annotations—Discussion of reported case and related cases; detailed discussions along lines of narrow topic.
Special Features	Sets: A.L.R. FED; A.L.R. 1st; A.L.R. 2nd; etc. Federal cases are reprinted and annotated in A.L.R. 1st and A.L.R. 2nd through1969. Since 1969, (select) federal cases are reprinted and annotated in A.L.R. FED.
Usefulness	Topics in A.L.R. are discrete—many important topics are not addressed at all.
Credibility	Very little authoritative value—do not quote from or cite.

g. Additional Secondary Authorities: Looseleaf Services, Practice Guides, and Form Books

Commercial Looseleaf Services	Specialized and administrative fields. Organized by area of law—often by agency or other responsible government entity. Common commercial publishers are CCH and BNA. Often publish daily issuances of federal administrative agencies.
Practice Guides	Most common for litigation practice and procedure. Useful practice guides include those that detail various federal rules and portions of Title 28 (see Chapter I.H.3.a. note 12).
Form Books	Organized by area of law and jurisdiction. Judicious use of form books can save time/money; should be accompanied by practitioner evaluation for each potential use and modification as may be necessary.

F. The Use of Precedent—The Principle of *Stare Decisis*

The use of court precedent—earlier court decisions in factually analogous cases—is one of the defining elements of the common law system. In short, the use of court precedent, known as the principle of *stare decisis,* requires that a court follow the rules of law established by the same or higher level courts in the same jurisdiction (see Chapter II.G.). Indeed, given the laudatory purposes served by the principle of *stare decisis* and its fundamental significance to our system of common law, many courts who are not required to follow precedent established in an earlier case will nevertheless apply the principle of *stare decisis.*

1. *Stare Decisis* Means "Let It [The Prior Decision] Stand"

Principle by which courts follow precedent (prior decisions in factually similar/analogous situations).

2. Rationale

   a. Judicial economy
   b. Fairness to parties
   c. Predictability
   d. Check on arbitrary behavior

3. Applies Only if Precedent is "Binding" or "Mandatory"

The principle of *stare decisis* does not apply to authority that is merely "persuasive."

4. Application of *Stare Decisis* Depends upon Two Main Factors

The determination whether the principle of *stare decisis* applies is based mainly on two factors: Jurisdiction and court level (hierarchy):

   a. *Jurisdiction*—The geographic region from which the case in question arose:
      (1)   State court? If so, which state?
      (2)   Federal court? If so, which district or circuit?[7]

   b. *Court Hierarchy*—The level of court from which the case arose:
      (1)   Trial level, appellate level, or court of last resort?

---

[7]   If the precedent was issued by the United States Supreme Court, that precedent will be treated as binding upon all courts, with one possible exception: If the Supreme Court precedent involved a matter of state law, it will not be binding upon the highest court of the relevant State. See Chapter II.G.

Jurisdiction and court level are critical to the application of *stare decisis* because the doctrine applies only with respect to cases decided within the same *jurisdiction* by a *higher level court.*

In addition, courts from the same jurisdiction are to consider and generally will follow precedent established at the same court level.*

Courts need not but may consider precedent established by courts in other jurisdictions.

5. Additional Factors to be Considered in Applying *Stare Decisis*
   a. Similarity of legal issue(s)
   b. Similarity of facts
   c. More recent precedent has greater persuasive value
   d. Whether precedent emerged from a court that the court at hand tends to follow or that is recognized as a leader in that subject area
   e. Whether precedent was well-reasoned

6. Importance to the Principle of *Stare Decisis* of Analogizing and Distinguishing Precedent

The application of *stare decisis* thus requires—in addition to a consideration of the jurisdiction and level of court of precedent—a consideration of the similarity between the issues of law and facts presented in the earlier case and those in the instant case. See Chapter II.D.

   a. *Analogizing:* If the court finds that the issues of law and fact are similar as a legal matter, then the court will likely analogize to the earlier case and apply the precedent to the later case.
   b. *Distinguishing:* If the court finds that the issues of law and/or fact are dissimilar from a legal perspective, then the court will probably not apply the precedent.

7. Deviations from the Principle of *Stare Decisis*

Despite the principle of *stare decisis,* courts will at times deviate (or appear to deviate) from earlier precedent.

The following points bear mentioning:

   a. Courts rarely explicitly overrule earlier applicable authority. Rather, they are more likely to distinguish facts or otherwise find that the earlier precedent does not apply on the merits.
   b. When courts recognize that earlier precedent in that jurisdiction should be overruled, they will rely on considerations such as the trend of other jurisdictions, newly developing policies, and the arcane nature of the earlier precedent.

---

* In the case of federal circuit courts, a panel is required to follow decisions rendered by another panel within the same circuit. See Chapter II.G.3.b.

c. A court can (but rarely does) overrule its own precedent, but a court may not overrule precedent established by a higher level court in that jurisdiction. Lower courts may indicate in their opinions their preference to rule in a manner contrary to precedent established by a higher level court, but only that higher level court is empowered to overrule earlier precedent.

G. Binding/Mandatory versus Persuasive Authority

Of the many sources of American law, some are considered to be "mandatory" or "binding," and others "persuasive."

While some sources of law are mandatory in some contexts, they may be merely persuasive in other contexts. For instance, a case that is binding on one court may not be binding on a court in another jurisdiction.

In addition, if authority is considered to be "persuasive," it does not mean that a subsequent court will consider it to be persuasive—only that the court *may* consider it in evaluating a case before it.

Mandatory/Binding Authority Defined	Authority a court must/is bound to follow.
Examples of Mandatory/Binding Authority	Applicable constitutions and statutes. Cases: General Rule— Holding (*i.e.*, not dictum); From a *higher level court;* In the *same jurisdiction;* In a *factually similar* case; Applying the *same law* (federal; particular state). See Chapter I.F.
Persuasive Authority Defined	Authority a court may, but is not required to, follow.
Examples of Persuasive Authority	Cases that are not binding (see above). Secondary sources. See Chapter I.E.2.

Factors Court May Use in Determining Whether to Consider and Apply Persuasive Authority	Jurisdiction Court hierarchy Factual similarities Policy Intervening authority Attractiveness of reasoning Date of prior authority Split among courts
Importance of Question Whether Authority is Mandatory or Persuasive	Relates to application of *stare decisis*. See Chapter I.F.

H. Federal and State Systems

1. Dual Federal and State Systems

The American legal system is based around a system of federalism, which basically refers to shared powers among the state and federal governments. The federal government is a government of limited powers, which are prescribed in the U.S. Constitution. The states retain all powers not expressly left exclusively to the federal government.

The federal government and most state governments have court systems based on three tiers. Cases proceed from the lowest level court to two separate levels of appeal. A few states have only a trial level court and one level of appeal.

(a) U.S. Government System Based on a System of Federalism
1. Shared powers between federal and state governments
2. Federal Constitution delegates to federal government specific powers; remaining powers are reserved for the states

(b) Federalism Results in Dual Court Systems
1. Federal court system
2. State court systems

(c) Consistent With Limited Power of Federal Government, Federal Courts Have Jurisdiction to Hear Cases Involving:
1. Federal constitutional issues
2. Federal statutory issues

3. Diversity cases—disputes between citizens of different states or of a citizen of a state against a citizen of a foreign country, if they meet a certain "jurisdictional amount" (currently $75,000, exclusive of costs)
4. Cases in which U.S. is a party
5. Other cases as specified by law—*e.g.,* admiralty, antitrust, maritime
6. Removal jurisdiction—if plaintiff could have brought case in federal court but brought case in state court, defendant can "remove" case to federal court, unless case is in defendant's home state

(d) State Courts May Review the Following Types of Cases

1. Any case, including those over which federal courts have jurisdiction
2. Exceptions to state court jurisdiction: State court jurisdiction may be precluded by federal statute either expressly (*e.g.,* admiralty, patent, copyright) or implicitly (*e.g.,* antitrust damages and injunctions)

(e) Typical Federal and State Court Structure

1. Three-tier structure is most typical
2. Three-tier structure:
   (a) Lower court—fact-finding
   (b) Intermediate court—appeals from lower court
   (c) High court—appeals from intermediate court

(f) Federal Court Structure

1. District Courts—Trial-Level Courts
   (a) Factual finding and development
   (b) Each state has one or more "districts" depending upon the size of the state
   (c) Several "districts" are combined to form one "circuit"
   (d) 94 districts form 12 circuits
2. Court Of Appeals—Intermediate Level Court
   (a) Appeals from trial-level (district) courts
   (b) Original jurisdiction over orders of many federal agencies
   (c) 13 circuit courts—one for each number 1-11; D.C. Circuit; Federal Circuit for certain specialized matters
   (d) Except for Federal Circuit, circuits are geographically-based

3. U.S. Supreme Court
    (a) Supreme court of the land
    (b) Original jurisdiction in very rare cases, *e.g.,* when there
         is a controversy between two states
    (c) Generally hears appeals from U.S. Court of Appeals
    (d) Hears some appeals from highest state courts
See Chapter I.H.3.

(g) State Court Structure

1. Most state court systems mirror that of the federal court sys-
    tem, *i.e.,* they generally are three-tiered, with two levels of
    appeal
2. Some states have only two-tiered court systems, with only one
    level of appeal
See Chapter I.H.4.

2. Illustration of the Dual American Court System

FEDERAL COURTS   **STATE COURTS**

Court Levels

U.S. Supreme Court   Court of last resort

U.S. Court of Appeals   Intermediate courts
[circuit courts]

U.S. District Courts   Trial courts

Court Jurisdiction

Federal Question [Statute/   Anything not
Constitution]   expressly or implicitly
                                                     reserved exclusively
                                                     for federal courts

Diversity

U.S. a party

Others as specified by law

Parallel Systems

A case will normally go through one system or another;
there is some overlap in unusual cases.

3. The Federal Courts: An Overview

The federal court system is a three-tiered system with one court of last resort (the U.S. Supreme Court, see chart immediately below), one intermediate court of appeals (the U.S. Court of Appeals, divided into 13 circuits, see Chapter I.H.3.b.), and a level of trial courts (the U.S. District Courts, of which there are 94, see Chapter I.H.3.c.). Several district courts are combined to form one circuit court.

a. United States Supreme Court

Formal Court Name	United States Supreme Court.[8]
Type Of Court	Court of last resort. Original jurisdiction in limited cases (*e.g.*, conflicts between states).
Basic Court Structure	One Supreme Court. Nine Justices. All justices hear and decide each case (unless recused/disqualified).[9]
Reporters	United States Reports—U.S. [official]. Supreme Court Reporter—S. Ct. [West]. Lawyers' Edition—L. Ed. [Lawyers' Cooperative]. United States Law Week/Supreme Court Bulletin—newest Court decisions.
Digests[10]	United States Supreme Court Digest [West]. Federal Practice Digest [currently in 4th series] [West]. Modern Federal Practice Digest [older cases] [West]. Federal Digest [older cases] [West].

---

8 Also referred to as the "Supreme Court" or the "Court" if it is clear from the context that the reference is to the United States Supreme Court.

9 Federal judges at all levels may be recused or disqualified for conflicts of interest (real or perceived) and other reasons. Grounds for disqualification are found at 28 U.S.C. § 455.

10 Reporters publish cases, while digests are a case finding tool. See Chapter II.A. and B.1.

Applicable Statutes And Rules	Rules of the United States Supreme Court.[11] Title 28 of the United States Code.[12]
Access To Court	Right of appeal: Limited classes of cases, generally involving state court declaration of unconstitutionality of federal law, federal court declaration of unconstitutionality of state laws, high state court upholding state law against claim of unconstitutionality. Original Jurisdiction: Involving ambassadors, controversies between states, etc. Petition for a *writ of certiorari:* Review completely discretionary with Supreme Court. Certification: Request by Court of Appeals that Supreme Court give instructions on a question of law. The Supreme Court may give binding instructions, or may hear the entire matter in controversy. Writ of Habeas Corpus: Limited right of redress for prisoners.[13]

b. United States Court of Appeals

Formal Court Name	United States Court of Appeals; United States Court of Appeals for the __ Circuit.[14]
Type Of Court	Intermediate court of appeals. Initial court review for some cases, especially appeals from agency action.

---

[11] All federal courts have their own rules of practice and procedure which should be consulted by the practitioner.

[12] Title 28 of the United States Code provides important information to the practitioner regarding many issues of federal court law, including issues of jurisdiction, venue, and other areas of federal court review. Title 28 should be consulted whenever an action is taken or planned to be taken in any federal court.

[13] A petition for a *writ of habeas corpus* should normally be filed in the first instance in a United States District Court. The Supreme Court will entertain an original request for the *writ* only under exceptional circumstances, including a showing that adequate relief can not be had in any other way.

[14] Also referred to as the "Court of Appeals for the __ Circuit," the "__ Circuit," the "court of appeals," or the "circuit court," if the reference is clear from the context. The term "circuit" comes from the old practice of circuit court judges to travel around the circuit to hear cases. Now, most appellate judges are assigned to a court in a single geographic location.

Basic Court Structure	Court of Appeals divided into 13 circuits: 1-11 (geographic), District of Columbia Circuit, Federal Circuit.[15] Each circuit (except Federal Circuit) comprised of one or more districts. Each circuit has varying number of judges, from six to twenty-eight, depending upon the size of the circuit and the volume of cases. Most cases heard and decided by 3-judge panel, selected at random.[16] Entire court may hear case *"en banc."* See Chapter V.B.
Reporter	Federal Reporter—F./F.2d./F.3d [West]
Digests	Federal Practice Digest [currently in 4th series] [West]. Modern Federal Practice Digest [older cases] [West]. Federal Digest [older cases] [West].
Applicable Statutes and Rules	Federal Rules of Appellate Procedure—applicable to all circuits. Local court rules adopted by and applicable within each circuit. See Fed. R. App. Proc. 47.[17] Local operating rules adopted by and applicable within each circuit. Title 28 of the United States Code.
Access to Court	Direct appeal from determinations of district courts. Direct review of final action of some federal agencies.

---

[15] Unlike the other circuit courts in which venue is based on geographic considerations, the Federal Circuit has jurisdiction over specialized matters, including intellectual property, international trade, government contracts, and other miscellaneous matters. The location and composition of each of the twelve geographic circuits may be found in a diagram in the front of each volume of the Federal Reporter and the Federal Supplement. See also 28 U.S.C. § 41.

[16] On occasion, a panel may not be selected at random if there is a particular reason to call a panel comprised of specific members. For instance, if a panel has already heard the same case and ordered a remand, the same panel may be assigned to hear that case on a renewed appeal or petition for review.

[17] See 28 U.S.C. § 2071.

c. United States District Courts

Formal Court Name	United States District Court [for the District of __].[18]
Type of Court	Trial court—deals with issues of fact, including motions relating to evidentiary and other matters.
Basic Court Structure	94 District Courts—one to four districts for each state.[19] Each District has a varying number of judges, from 1-28. Cases heard by a single judge.[20] Cases may be, but are rarely, heard *en banc*.
Reporters	Federal Supplement—F. Supp. [West]. Federal Rules Decisions (selected district court cases on procedural issues)—FRD [West].
Digests	Federal Practice Digest [currently in 4th series] [West]. Modern Federal Practice Digest [older cases] [West]. Federal Digest [older cases] [West].
Applicable Statutes and Rules	Federal Rules of Civil Procedure. Federal Rules of Evidence. Local court rules adopted by and applicable within each district. See Fed. R. Civ. Proc. 83.[21] Title 28 of the United States Code.
Access to Court	Initial level of court review.
Other "Courts" at Level Similar to District Courts	U.S. Tax Court. U.S. Bankruptcy Court. Judicial Panel on Multidistrict Litigation.

---

[18] If the district is the only one in a particular state, the name of the district will be the abbreviation of that state's name [D. Ariz.]. If a state has more than one district, the district will have a geographical designation accompanying the abbreviation of the name of the state [S.D. N.Y.]. Also referred to as "district court" if the reference is clear from the context.

[19] See 28 U.S.C. §§ 81-131 for the location of and distribution of districts among the states.

[20] Even though cases are heard by a single judge, reference to "the court" is preferred to reference to "the judge."

[21] See also 28 U.S.C. § 2071.

4. The State Courts: An Overview

a. State Court Structure For the most part, state court systems are analogous to the federal court system in that they have three-tiered structures: a trial court, an intermediate court of appeal, and a court of last resort (a supreme court). A few states have only one appellate-level court.

At the trial court level, there may be divisions or departments for specialized matters such as family issues, probate, and juvenile matters.

Many states also have inferior courts, which are not courts of record but are very informal and handle lesser forms of recovery, such as small claims court.

States are often separated into districts or other geographic divisions for purposes of court allocation. These districts operate much like—but are completely distinct from—federal districts.

b. State Reporter Systems Each state has either and/or an official or a West case reporter which report intermediate appellate and high court cases.*

Most states' appellate and high court opinions are also published in West regional reporters, which combine the published cases of several states into West "regions." [Note: the combination of states together in a West regional digest has no bearing on the relative precedential value of the cases from the states that happen to be combined by a commercial entity (West) into a single regional reporter. These regions and the states that form them have nothing to do with jurisdiction or anything else other than the convenience of the publisher.]

The most efficient way to learn which reporters contain the opinions of a particular state court is to consult Table T.1 of the Bluebook. See Chapter IX.

c. State Court Digests Each state has its own digest.

Some state digests are published by West; other states have digests that are published by another private company or by the state itself.

Some states have a West digest *and* a digest published by some other entity.

Many published state cases are also digested in one of the West regional digests.

---

* Most trial court decisions are not published because such decisions often take the form of jury verdicts which, have no precedential value in subsequent litigation.

d. State Court Rules of Practice and Procedure   Each state also has its own rules of practice and procedure applicable to each court. Most states will have annotated versions of their rules of practice and procedure, or practice guides describing the application of such rules.

I.   Interrelationship Among Sources of Law

1. Interrelationship Among Federal Government Institutions

a. Three Branches of Government   The American federal government is comprised of three branches of government—the legislative branch, the executive branch, and the judicial branch. Each arm of the federal government has unique functions and responsibilities.

b. Federal System of Checks and Balances   The federal government was designed with a system of "checks and balances," in which each branch in some way acts as a restraint on the other branches. For the practitioner's purposes, the judicial oversight function over the legislative branch is most significant.[22]

c. Authority of Federal Courts   Federal courts have the authority to review acts of Congress for their constitutionality. When an act of Congress establishes and/or authorizes an agency to take action, court review may include the question of whether that delegation of authority is constitutional.

Federal courts also have the authority to review actions of administrative agencies. Inquiries a court may make of agency action include whether the agency has acted in a manner consistent with the authority granted by Congress to the agency; whether the agency's actions are consistent with other statues;[23] and whether the agency's actions are consistent with prior court and agency decisions.[24]

---

[22] Other examples of checks and balances built into the federal system include congressional oversight of the executive and executive oversight over Congress. For instance, the Senate has the authority to try the President and other executives who are impeached (brought up on charges) by the House, and to approve certain presidential nominations. The President, for his part, has the authority to veto legislation passed by Congress. See Chapter III.D.

[23] Under the U.S. Constitution, Congress is charged with law-making authority. To the extent Congress is seen to have delegated excessive law-making authority to an agency (or, for that matter, any other entity), a court will invalidate such delegation. Invalidation of an act of Congress on this ground is rare, but remains a potential source of judicial inquiry of which to be aware.

[24] While agencies are not bound by strict principles of *stare decisis,* they are generally required to explain departures from earlier decisions. As for rulemaking, agencies are required to explain the need for changes to existing rules.

d. Congressional Authority To "Overrule" Court Precedent Prospectively

While the Supreme Court is largely considered to have the "last word" on the legality of acts of Congress and actions of federal agencies, Congress has authority to "overrule" or modify *prospectively* through legislation even Supreme Court precedent. But Congress cannot "overrule" a constitutional decision.

For instance, if a court has held that an agency acted beyond its statutory authority, Congress can amend the relevant legislation to more explicitly authorize the agency to take the action in question. However, if the Supreme Court holds that legislation to be unconstitutional, only a constitutional amendment can override that decision.[26]

2. The Judicial Review Function: The Interrelationship Between Congress and the Federal Courts

ACTS OF U.S. CONGRESS		FEDERAL COURT REVIEW FUNCTION
Passes laws	→	Is law constitutional?
Creates and authorizes agencies to act	→	Is delegation to agency constitutional?
ADMINISTRATIVE AGENCIES		
Issue rules and regulations	→	Is action consistent with Constitution?
Resolve disputes via adjudications	→	Is action consistent with congressional delegation and other laws?[25]
	→	Is action consistent with case law?

CONGRESS
[Prospective Only][27]
Codify case law
Modify/amend case law
Reject/"overrule" case law
  (unless based on
  constitutional infirmity)

---

[25] Agency authority is generally derived from specific statutory authority to that agency. Agency actions are also governed by the Administrative Procedure Act, a more generic statutory scheme applicable to federal agencies generally.

[26] A constitutional amendment requires a proposal by two-thirds of both houses of Congress, or two-thirds of the state legislatures, and ratification by three-quarters of the state legislatures.

[27] These actions of Congress, in turn, would likewise be subject to judicial review.

3. Relative Priority of Sources of Law: Hierarchy of Authority

In any given legal situation, many sources of law may be applicable. For instance, a case may present a federal constitutional issue, but may also implicate issues of statutory law (state or federal). There is a complex reaction to the issue of which law has "supremacy" over others.

First, there is the issue of federal supremacy over state law. A complex area of jurisprudence, this principle basically stands for the proposition that when there is conflict between a federal law and a state law, federal law supersedes the state law. In addition, there are certain fields over which federal law preempts the possibility of any state law.

In addition, even within the federal system or a state system, there are rules of supremacy governing the relative priority of sources of law applicable *within that jurisdiction.* As indicated below, the U.S. Constitution takes priority over federal statutes and regulations, which in turn take priority over federal case law. The U.S. Constitution, of course, also takes priority over state statutes, regulations, and case law.

It is critical that case law be examined *whenever* interpreting a statutory or constitutional provision. As an example, consider the sources of federal law: Although the U.S. Constitution and then federal statutes take priority (under the principles of constitutional supremacy and legislative supremacy, respectively) in interpreting the Constitution or a statute, case law will be critical; under the principle of *stare decisis,* the way in which the same or similar constitutional and statutory provisions have been interpreted in the past will have an enormous impact on the way in which a constitutional or statutory provision will be interpreted.

a. Federal Law

    (1) U.S. Constitution
    (2) Federal Statutes
    (3) Federal Rules and Regulations
    (4) Federal Cases—Cases must be consulted in interpreting Constitution, statutes, and agency issuances

b. State Law

There are several principles of law that must be considered when dealing with an issue of state law. Although a comprehensive examination of these rather complex rules is beyond the scope of this work, they are as follows:

(1) *Federal Supremacy:*
Federal law prevails over conflicting state law. State law may not be inconsistent with federal law. Nor may there be state laws covering areas that have been preempted, or fully covered, by a federal statutory scheme.

(2) Erie* *Rule:*
Federal courts will apply state "substantive" law (*e.g.,* torts, contracts) and federal "procedural" law when state law creates the cause of action.

(3) *Choice of Law Issues:*
A federal court deciding which state's law to apply to a state claim will use the choice of law rules of the state in which the federal court sits.

Apart from these issues, the following hierarchy of authority would apply to state sources of law:

(1) State Constitution
(2) State Statutes
(3) State Rules and Regulations
(4) State Cases—Must be consulted in interpreting state Constitution, statutes, and agency issuances

A Note On Citations To Authority: When citing to federal or state law, citations should include all relevant sources, in the order of their respective hierarchy. See Chapter IX.C.

---

* *Erie R. Co. v. Tompkins,* 304 U.S. 64 (1938).

CHAPTER II

CASE LAW

A. Anatomy of a Case—Case Reporters

1. Case Format [West Reporters[28]]

Informal Case Name/Citation	At top of page. Cite is normally not consistent with *Bluebook* form. See Chapter IX.
Caption	Indicates names of parties (at trial level, plaintiff appears first; on appeal, appellant/petitioner usually appears first). May not be in proper *Bluebook* form. See Chapter IX.
Court	Name/division of court issuing opinion.
Date	Relevant date is date of opinion, not date of oral argument.
Synopsis/Syllabus	Useful summary of case. Written by publisher of reporter. Should *never* be quoted, cited, or relied upon.*

---

[28] Most published federal cases and many state cases appear in West reporters. For instance, all published federal district court cases, federal appellate court cases, and U.S. Supreme Court cases are found in West reporters. In addition, most published state decisions are also reported in either a West state reporter and/or a West regional reporter. See Chapter I.H.3. and 4. Published cases that are not printed by West tend to be in a similar format.

The most significant departure involves the lack of the West headnote system in non-West publications. Non-West publications, however, may have their own headnotes, but those headnotes will not be accessible through the West Digest system. See Chapter II.A.2. and B.1.

* In some states, there is an exception to this general rule in that the syllabus represents the black letter holding of the case and is considered to be definitive authority.

Headnotes [See "Dissecting A West Headnote," Below]	Written by publisher of reporter. Should *never* be quoted, cited, or relied upon. See note 28. Useful in finding portions of opinion in which particular issues are addressed. Contents of headnote: • Number—corresponds to portion of case in brackets [ ] at which that topic will be addressed. • Topic/Key number—place in West Digest where cites to cases on this issue will be found. • Blurb—West editorial description of what the corresponding part of the opinion says.
Author	Name of judge writing majority opinion. Name(s) of concurring/dissenting judges may also be indicated. See Chapter VIII.B.3.
Judges	Names of judges on panel, if more than one (usually the situation in appeals).
Counsel	Name of counsel for the parties.
Opinion of the Court	Opinion of the majority of the court. See Chapter VIII.B.3.
Separate Opinions	Concurring opinion(s)—disagree with reasoning but agree with result reached in the majority opinion. Dissenting opinion(s)—disagree with the outcome and reasoning of the majority opinion. See Chapter VIII.B.3.

2. Dissecting a West Headnote[29]

Number	Corresponds to number in opinion in brackets [ ] immediately preceding portion of case corresponding to that headnote.
Topic	West Digest Topic where reader will find citations to cases referring to issue/subject discussed in the blurb.
Key Number	Sub-Part under Topic in West Digest where citations to cases discussing this particular point will be found.
Blurb	West editorial description of what the corresponding part of the opinion says.

Number   Topic   Key Number
   ↑   ↑   ↑
Example: **8. Contracts**   **28(1)**
Parties are presumed to have entered into valid and binding
contract. → *Blurb*

B. Working With Case Law

The remainder of this chapter deals with researching case law that
may or may not have a statutory or constitutional component. When a legal
issue is governed by a federal statute or constitutional provision, there are
other resources to use in finding applicable cases. See Chapter III.B.

1. Use of West Digest System to Find a Case

a. What is the West Digest System?   The West Digest system is
a very useful way to locate cases.

b. Digests as a Form of Secondary Authority   Digests are simply
finding tools, which allow the user to locate cases.

Digests are a form of secondary authority, in that they are tools that
may be used to locate primary authority.

Digests are different from other secondary sources (see Chapter
I.E.2.), because they do not have any persuasive authority and may not be
cited for any reason.

---

[29] For a discussion of the use of the West Headnote system, see Chapter II.B.1.

c. Digests as Differentiated from Reporters   It is important to keep in mind the distinction between digests and reporters.

Digests are case finding tools that enable the reader to locate cases.

Reporters are the volumes that contain the cases themselves.

d. West Topics and Key Numbers Are Consistent across all West Digests   As described in the chart below, West Digests are accessed through a series of Topics and Key numbers, which represent specific issues. A West topic, along with its Key number, may be referred to as a Headnote.

The West Topic and Key number system is particularly useful in that the Topics and Key numbers are consistent across all Digest sets (representing different jurisdictions) and series (representing Digests over time).

What is the West Digest System?	Digest of cases organized around an index organized by subject/topic.
What are Digests used for?	Digests allow the user to locate cases on a particular issue or topic.
	Digests themselves do not contain cases, but provide blurbs about cases and provide the citation to the case reporter where that case itself may be found.
Organization of West Digests	Organized by jurisdiction and chrono-logically.
	Jurisdictional organization ["Sets"]:
	• Federal Practice Digest—all federal cases from all levels.
	• Regional Digests—by West regions.
	• State Digests—for selected states.
	• Decennial Digests—combined state and federal digests for ten year periods.

Organization of Digests (cont'd)	• General Digests—non-cumulative updates to Decennial Digests. Chronological organization ["Series"]: • Each digest set proceeds to 2d, 3d, 4th series, etc. • Only distinction among series is the time frame covered by each series. • Higher numbered series digest newer cases than the lower numbered series, or those with no number.
How to Update Digests	Pocket parts and/or paperbound supplements are published for each West Digest volume. Those volumes with no pocket part or supplement should so indicate in the back inside cover.
How to Use Digests	*Pick a topic*—West Digests list topics found therein. A more experienced practitioner may know what topic to refer to for a specific issue. *Go to that topic*—topics are located alphabetically in the digest volumes. *Review outline under your chosen topic*—longer topics will normally have a broad outline and a more detailed outline of specific issues within that topic. *Select potentially relevant headnotes to review*—each entry on the outline is represented by a "key" number, under which there will be case digests to the issue selected. *Caution:* do not stop when you have found one relevant "key" number in the Digest. Cases relevant to your issue may appear under any number of West Digest topics and/or key numbers.

"Sets" of Digests	A *set* refers to digests by jurisdiction(s) represented therein.
"Series" of Digests	A *series* refers to the chronological order of the various sets. Higher numbered series digest newer cases, while lower numbered series digest older cases.
West Key Numbers are Consistent Among All Sets and Series of West Digests.	West Key numbers are consistent among all digests from all jurisdictions and among all series. [Note: Some changes have been made over the years, and are so indicated at the beginning of any Topic containing changed Key numbers.] Thus, once you have found a relevant Topic and Key number in one digest, that same number may be used to update older digests through the pocket part/supplement; in looking in older digest sets; or in looking in other sets of digests.
A Note About Citations in Digests	Citations to cases in West Digests are not consistent with *Bluebook* form. See Chapter IX.

2. Shepard's Citators

Shepard's Citators is a commercial service that allows the user to update cases found by finding other cases (and other authorities) that cite to a given case, and to learn whether a given case was reversed or over-ruled.

Although Shepard's Citators is discussed below in the context of case law, there are Shepard's Citators for many other sources of law. See note 30. Like digests, Shepard's Citators are finding tools, and may not be quoted, cited, or relied upon.

What is Shepard's Citators?	Service that provides citations to all cases and select other authorities to which a given case (or other authority)[30] cites.
How to Shepardize a Given Case [Case X]	Choose Shepard's volume(s) containing Case X [based on time/jurisdiction]. Find Case X in Shepard's volumes selected by its citation. [Note: Newer Shepard's volumes contain the name of Case X with its citation.] Entries under Case X will represent page numbers of cases and other authorities at which Case X is cited.
What Information Shepard's Provides	Case X history and verification—further action on remand or appeal. Case X treatment—cites to subsequent authorities citing Case X. Superscript numbers after citation indicate headnote number of Case X to which cited case refers. Letters to the left of citations to subsequent authority indicate case history and treatment; a list in the front of every Shepard's volume translates these letters. Parallel citations for Case X—citations to Case X as it appears in other reporters.
Purposes of Shepard's Citators	Case verification—is Case X still good law? Has a higher court made a disposition of Case X? Case treatment—what have other cases said about Case X? Helps to interpret Case X. Case research—finding other cases that bear on research issue. Parallel Citations.

---

[30] In addition to reported state and federal decisions, Shepard's Citators are available for statutes, the U.S. Constitution, the Code of Federal Regulations (C.F.R.), court rules, select administrative decisions, restatements, law reviews, and other assorted publications. Their most common use, however, is for cases.

3. General Research Strategy

The following chart demonstrates ways to get started in defining a traditional research goal and executing initial research steps. The chart that follows (Chapter II.B.4.) provides more detailed information for completing case research.

Goal Definition—Find Cases in the Following Order of Priority:	Mandatory authority on point; or Mandatory authority useful by analogy; or Persuasive authority on point; or Persuasive authority useful by analogy.
Through Descriptive Words	West Digest Topic Index/Words and Phrases/Descriptive Word Index $\rightarrow$ West Digest. Am. Jur. Index $\rightarrow$ Am. Jur. C.J.S. Index $\rightarrow$ C.J.S. A.L.R. Word Index $\rightarrow$ A.L.R. Annotations. **All above lead to cases.**
Through Area of Law	Treatises. Restatement. West Digest. Hornbooks. Am. Jur./C.J.S. **All above lead to cases.**
Through a Known Case	West Digest through Headnote from known case. Shepard's Citators. A.L.R. case table. Other cases cited in known case. **All above lead to cases.**

4. Using Known Information to Find Additional Cases

The following chart is a more comprehensive and detailed description of ways in which you might execute a research strategy. In particular, depending upon the information you already have concerning your legal issue, this chart helps you to find other cases involving the same issue, and shows how that information may be used in conjunction with other resources.

Source You Have	Go To	How to Use Found Resources
Known Relevant Case	Other [older] cases cited therein. West Headnotes. Shepard's Citators	Read earlier cases. Go to West Digest to find additional cases under that Headnote topic and key numbers. Read cases cited. **All above lead to additional cases.**
Topic or Subject	West Analysis and Topic Outlines. West Words and Phrases. West Descriptive-Word Index. Restatement.	Topic Outlines lead to West Digest to find cases under that Headnote topic and key number. Words and Phrases will lead to case cites. Descriptive-Word Index leads to references to Digest topics and key numbers. Case citations and digests in appendix volumes. **All above lead to additional cases.**
West Subject and Key Number	West Digest, including Pocket Part/Supplement.	Leads you to cases relating to that topic and key number. Use Headnotes in cases to refer you to Digest topics and key numbers. **All above lead to additional cases.**
Secondary Authorities	Cases cited therein.	Read cases. Use Headnotes in cases to refer you to Digest topics and key numbers. **All above lead to additional cases.**
Shepard's Citators	Cases cited therein.	Read cases. Use Headnotes in cases to refer you to Digest topics and key numbers. **All above lead to additional cases.**
Plaintiff's Name Only	West Table of Cases.	Case citation. Use Headnotes in cases to refer you to Digest topics and key numbers. **All above lead to additional cases.**
Defendant's Name Only	West Digest Defendant-Plaintiff Table of Cases.	Case citation. Use Headnotes in cases to refer you to Digest topics and key numbers. **All above lead to additional cases.**

5. Updating Case Law

As with all authority to which you cite or rely in research, it is critical to ensure that you have updated your research. This is important for at least two reasons. First, it is imperative that you know whether a case upon which you intend to rely has been overruled (subsequent case treatment) or reversed (subsequent case history). Second, the persuasive effect of your work will be heightened by using the most current applicable case law.

The chart below demonstrates how to update case law.

If You Have	Use This to Update
Case	Shepard's Citators. Advance Sheets. Slip Opinions.
Finding Tools (e.g., Digest)	Pocket Parts, Paperbound Supplements.
Secondary Authority	Pocket Parts, Paperbound Supplements.

6. Summary of Case Law Research: Tools and Sources of Verification and Update

The following chart is a compilation of sources of case law and the various case finding tools and mechanisms by which to verify and update case law. It also indicates whether each source listed is primary authority or secondary authority, or whether the source itself has no authoritative value itself but is only a case finding tool.

Sources of Case Law	Case Finding Tools*	Case Verification/ Update
Reporters [1] • Federal (U.S. Reports/ Federal Reports/ Federal Supplement) • State • Regional See also Chapter VIII.A.	West Digest [0] • Federal • State • Regional • Decennial • General	Digest Pocket Parts/ Supplements [0]
	Known cases [1]	Shepard's Citators [0]
	Shepard's Citators [0]	Shepard's updates [0]
	Encyclopedias [2] • Am. Jur. • C.J.S.	Encyclopedia Pocket Parts/ Supplements [2]
	Treatises [2]	Treatise Pocket Parts/ Supplements [2]
	Hornbooks [2]	New Editions of Hornbook [2]
	Restatements [2]	Appendix Volumes [2] Interim Case Citations [0] Pocket Parts/Supplements [2]
	A.L.R. Annotations [2]	A.L.R. Pocket Parts/ Supplements [2]
	Law Reviews [2]	Shepard's Citators [0]

[1] = Primary Authority
[2] = Secondary Authority
[0] = Not authority—finding tool only

* See also Chapter III.B. for a discussion on finding cases when a federal statutory or constitutional provision is involved.

C. Identifying and Working With Dictum

Dictum *(pl. dicta)* Defined: Roughly speaking, dictum is that part of the court's decision that was not necessary to the court's resolution of the issue before it.

Some Important Points About Dictum:

- Dictum is not always easy to identify or distinguish from the court's holding.

- Dictum is not a particularly laudable object; as a result, many cases will not discuss issues that are not directly before it.

- While dictum is not part of the court's holding, and it is not mandatory authority, it may be used either by litigants or by courts in later cases as authority for the proposition represented by the dictum.

COMPARING HOLDING AND DICTUM

	HOLDING *(ratio decidendi)*	DICTUM *(obiter dictum)*
Defining Characteristics	Rule of law from a decision. Judgment plus material facts of a case. Analysis of material facts, decision, and reasoning of court. Summary of case-specific facts and relevant legal consequences.	Statements and commentary not essential to the court's resolution of the precise issue(s) presented for decision. Issues and/or facts not before court.
Persuasive Effect on Subsequent Court Decisions	Binding, so long as other requirements for binding effect apply. See Chapter I.F.	Never binding on any court, but may be persuasive. Worthy of respect by parties and courts.
Reasons for Relative Persuasive Effect on Subsequent Court Decisions	Limited jurisdiction of court to decide only those issues presented by the parties and situations before it. Dedication to judicial role of deciding only issues and facts brought to it for resolution and dedication to notions of advocacy.	Concern that court may not have fully considered issues related to dictum when not brought before court by parties with standing and live controversies including specific facts and/or issues. Reliance on advocates.
Treatment of Facts	Based on facts actually brought before the court.	Based on hypothetical facts or facts that are a variation from facts brought before court by the parties.
Treatment of Legal Issues	Based on legal issues actually brought before the court.	Based on hypothetical issues or those that are a variation from issues brought before court by the parties.
Effect on Parties' Strategic Decisions In Later Cases	May try to broaden or narrow court's "holding" to apply to or be distinguished from present case. Parties will represent breadth of "holding" as narrow or broad depending upon their position vis-a-vis that holding in subsequent cases.	May use dictum as a way of encouraging court to apply dictum to present case, either by arguing that reasoning follows so closely from holding that it cannot be distinguished from holding, or that dictum is persuasive authority that the court ought to adopt.

D. Analogizing and Distinguishing Cases

Legal analysis often involves analogizing to and distinguishing from existing precedent. For instance, in arguing that a holding in a certain case is applicable to your case, you would try to analogize your case to that earlier case.

On the other hand, in arguing that the holding of a particular case does not compel the same result in your case, you would try to distinguish the earlier case from your case.

In determining whether precedent is binding, a court will also analogize to and distinguish the case at hand from the precedent. See Chapter I.F.6.

1. Analogize: Argue *in Favor* of Application of Precedent
  a. Material facts similar enough to warrant same result.
  b. Depict holding as broad.
  c. Legal issue(s) same or substantially similar.
  d. Similar policy reasons warrant same result.

2. Distinguish: Argue *Against* Application of Precedent
  a. Material facts different.
  b. Depict holding as narrow.
  c. Legal issue(s) not sufficiently similar.
  d. Sound policy supports different result.

E. Dealing With Contrary Authority

The practitioner may find that there is contrary authority that may affect the outcome of a case. When this occurs, the practitioner has several possible responses.

1. Ethical Obligation to Reveal Contrary Authority

As a preliminary matter—one that comes as a surprise to many—an attorney has an ethical obligation to reveal to the court contrary authority that is binding on the court.

This principle, however, does not often operate to require one side to reveal contrary authority to the court. First, it can reasonably be expected (assuming even a minimal level of competence), that one's opponent will locate and use legal authority in favor of his or her client. Second, "contrary authority" is really a rather narrow term—one that implies that the authority is directly on point and that assumes a virtual likeness between the facts and legal issues presented. Thus, finding authority that can be said to be truly "contrary" is not a common likelihood.

2. How to Negate or Minimize the Importance of Contrary Authority

The more common scenario that you are likely to face is one in which your opponents identify authority they assert undermines the strength of your position. There are several strategies for minimizing the impact of such a claim. For instance, the following arguments (roughly in order of persuasiveness) may be made:

    a. The facts are distinguishable and therefore not applicable to the case at hand.

    b. The legal issues differ.

    c. The so-called contrary authority is not binding on the court before which you appear or will appear.

    d. The earlier precedent, while not directly overruled, has been effectively repudiated by the court that issued it.

    e. The weight of authority in other jurisdictions supports a contrary result.

    f. Policy issues now support a change in the law.

3. When and How to Acknowledge Contrary Authority

a. In an Interoffice Memorandum   In writing an interoffice memorandum of law (see Chapter X.), any arguably contrary authority must, of course, be revealed and discussed. If there is a way to distinguish that authority, or to otherwise argue that it is inapplicable to the present case, the attorney should do so. If the authority is truly contrary and there is no viable way to negate its importance to the client's position, the lawyer must also so indicate. The presence of contrary authority, of course, will have an enormous impact on strategy decisions, including settlement possibilities.

b. In Writings to the Court   In writings to the court, the best approach is normally to reveal potentially contrary authority before your opponent does so. There are several effective ways to do so:

    1. Present the authority in a way that minimizes its negative impact to the extent possible.

    2. Appear to be unafraid of disclosing the potentially damaging authority.

3. Juxtapose the potentially contrary authority with an argument as to why it should not be the basis for an unfortunate ruling in your case.

F. Terminology Relating to Court and Party Usage

There is a range of terminology used in the law. Some of the basic terms used by lawyers and attorneys are set forth in other sections of this book. See Chapters III., IV., V., VI., VII. and VIII.

Set forth below are some terms traditionally used by courts and practitioners, but which are frequently misunderstood and, as a result, misused and misapplied.

Terms Used by Courts	What They Mean
Facts	Facts are "presented" by the parties (through counsel). Facts are "found" by the court (*e.g.,* "The court *found* that the plaintiff's reliance on the defendant's representations was reasonable).
Laws/Rules Of Law	Laws/Rules of Law are "held" (*e.g.,* the court *held* that the defendant's misrepresentations were actionable).
Reverse	Higher level court "reverses" the decision of a lower court in the *same* litigation. Reversal of a case involves the same case and the same parties on appeal from a lower level court.
Overrule	Court in *subsequent* litigation "overrules" a rule of law that was announced in earlier, different litigation involving different parties.
Deny	A court may *deny* [refuse to order the relief requested in] a motion.
Grant	A court may *grant* [order the relief requested in] a motion.
Affirm	A court may *affirm* [uphold] the holding of a lower court.
Decide	A court may *decide* [issue a ruling on] a case or a motion.

Important terms that are used by *parties:* contend, argue, allege, oppose, favor, and the like.

G. Precedential Effect of Case Law and the Application of *Stare Decisis*

1. Introduction

There are two basic questions that are central to the question of the impact, or "precedential value," of one case upon a later case. They are (a) court hierarchy, and (b) jurisdiction. The question of precedential effect of one case upon later cases, of course, is directly related to the principle of *stare decisis,* discussed in more general terms earlier in this book. See Chapter I.F.

a. Court Hierarchy Court hierarchy has to do with the "level" of court—trial; intermediate/appellate; supreme court/court of last resort.

Generally speaking, decisions of a higher level court within the same jurisdiction will have a binding or mandatory effect on lower level courts within that same jurisdiction.

b. Jurisdiction Jurisdiction in this context has to do with the place from which the decision arose. In particular, jurisdiction involves the following two questions:

(1) Whether the case was decided in federal or state court; *and*
(2) Which federal or state court:
    (a) If federal court: Which circuit or district?[31]
    (b) If state court: Which state?

Generally speaking, a case has mandatory precedential value only within the same federal district, federal circuit or state.

2. General Rules Regarding Precedential Effect and the Application of *Stare Decisis*

a. General Rules Re: Federal Law

- Pronouncements of U.S. Supreme Court binding on all courts.
- Pronouncements of U.S. circuit courts binding within that circuit court and all district courts within that circuit. Not binding on state courts, although highly persuasive.[32]

---

[31] Pronouncements of the U.S. Supreme Court on matters of federal law are binding on *all* courts, state and federal.

[32] Many students find it surprising that state courts are not bound by interpretations of federal law by U.S. district or circuit courts. However, most state courts would find highly persuasive decisions of federal courts, especially those within the district or circuit within which those states sit.

- Pronouncements of highest state court binding on all courts in that state.
- Pronouncements of lower level state courts binding on that court and lower state courts only.
- Pronouncements of U.S. district courts are not binding on other judges, although other judges in that district should look to that decision as persuasive authority.

b. General Rules Re: State Law

- Pronouncements of highest state court binding on all courts (state and federal) interpreting that state's law.
- Pronouncements of intermediate level state courts binding on that court and lower level state courts.
- Pronouncements of U.S. circuit court binding on that circuit and all district courts within that circuit, but not on the state courts of the state at issue.
- Pronouncements of U.S. Supreme Court binding on all courts, except highest state court.

It should, of course, be recalled that the precedential value of an earlier court ruling is dependent upon the extent to which the court in the later case views the earlier case as factually similar and otherwise apposite to the case at hand. See Chapter I.F.

3. Precedential Effect of Court Rulings on Federal Law: General Rules

a. Precedential Effect of Rulings of the United States Supreme Court

(1) All Federal courts must follow the directives of the United States Supreme Court.

(2) The United States Supreme Court will generally follow its own directives under the principle of *stare decisis.* The Supreme Court—and only the Supreme Court—may overrule earlier opinions of the Court.

(3) State courts must follow the directives of the Supreme Court when those directives implicate a federal statutory or constitutional provision or right.

b. Precedential Effect of Rulings of the United States Court of Appeals

(1) A panel of a circuit court is required to follow precedent established by any panel of that circuit.

(2) A circuit court may overrule precedent established by a panel of that circuit only through an *en banc*[33] opinion of that court. See Chapter VI.B.

(3) A court of appeals is not required to follow precedent established by another circuit court, although it may look to rulings of sister circuits and find that authority persuasive.

(4) A district court is required to follow precedent established by the appeals court of the circuit in which it sits.

(5) A district court is not required to follow precedent established by another circuit or by other district courts, either within or outside of the circuit in which it sits. See below.

c. Precedential Effect of Rulings of the United States District Courts

(1) A district court is not required to follow precedent established by another district court judge, but a district court judge is to consider precedent established by other judges within that district.

(2) Under principles of comity, a district court is not required to but may look towards rulings of other district courts and may find that precedent to be persuasive. District courts tend to do this especially when a novel legal issue is being decided.

d. Precedential Effect of Rulings of State Courts[34]

(1) All federal courts and courts in other states ("other" courts) interpreting a state law must "stand in the shoes" of the highest court of that state and apply that state's law as they believe that court would apply it.

(2) If the highest court of the state has not spoken to the issue involved, the "other" court must try to predict what the ruling of such court would be were it to rule on the issue. In making this prediction, the "other" court will look for guidance to the lower court opinions of that state, but the "other" court may conclude that the high state court would have reached a contrary conclusion.

---

[33] *En banc* opinions are opinions by all judges on an appeals court sitting together as a whole as opposed to the usual three-judge panel. See Chapter VI.B.

[34] Under the *Erie* doctrine and its progeny, state court precedent is important to a federal court disposition of an issue whenever state substantive law is at issue in a case brought in federal court. See Chapter I.I.3.b.

(3) If the high state court has already spoken on the issue, the "other" court may even conclude that that court would now rule differently, although such a conclusion would be extremely rare.

e. Precedential Effect of Federal Court Decisions on Matters of Federal Law

Precedent Established By:	In Subsequent Opinion By:	Precedential Effect:
U.S. Supreme Court	U.S. Supreme Court	Tendency to follow under *stare decisis*
	Any Federal Circuit Court	Binding
	Any Federal District Court	Binding
	Any State Court	Binding
U.S. Court Of Appeals, Cir. X	U.S. Supreme Court	Not binding
	U.S. Court of Appeals, Cir. X	Binding; overturn only by *en banc* decision[35]
	U.S. Court of Appeals, Not Cir. X	Not binding
	U.S. District Court Within Cir. X	Binding
	U.S. District Court Not Within Cir. X	Not Binding
	State Court in State Within Cir. X	Not Binding
	State Court in State Not Within Cir. X	Not Binding
U.S. District Court, Dist. A	U.S. Supreme Court	Not binding
	U.S. Court of Appeals, Any Circuit	Not binding
	U.S. District Court, Dist. A	Not binding, but must be considered
	U.S. District Court, Not Dist. A	Not binding
	State Court Within Dist. A	Not binding
	State Court Not Within Dist. A	Not binding

---

[35] See Chapter VI.B.

CHAPTER III

STATUTES AND LEGISLATIVE HISTORY

A. Preliminary Points Relating to Federal Statutes and Legislative History

1. Congress: A Bicameral Institution

The U.S. Congress is a bicameral institution created by the United States Constitution, comprised of the Senate and the House of Representatives.

2. The House of Representatives

The House of Representatives is the so-called "lower" house. It is considered to be more representative of the people, because the number of representatives is based on the population of each state. The states are divided into congressional districts, with each district electing one representative. Each representative serves a two-year term, with re-election possible for an infinite number of terms. The House has certain exclusive powers such as the power to impeach (bring up on charges) the President and other federal officers and federal judges. In addition, spending legislation must be initiated in the House.

3. The Senate

The Senate is considered to be the "higher" chamber, and is more representative of the states, given that each of the 50 states elects two Senators. Senators serve 6-year terms, also with the possibility of re-election. Senators have certain powers that the members of the House do not have. For instance, the Senate ratifies treaties, confirms major presidential appointees, and tries impeached parties.

4. How Laws Are Passed

Laws, or statutes, are passed by a majority of each chamber of Congress and signed into law by the President.[36]

---

[36] A bill may become law without the approval of the President. If the President does not sign legislation within 10 days after being passed by Congress and time remains in the congressional session, that bill becomes law. If the President vetoes a law passed by Congress, Congress may override that veto with a two-thirds vote of each chamber of Congress. See Chapter III.D.

5. Legislative Supremacy

Statutes take precedent over cases, but (as indicated below) cases must be consulted in interpreting a statute. Statutes are often vague and ambiguous and courts are therefore often called upon to decide what a statute means. This body of case law becomes part of the "law" of the statute, and must be consulted whenever considering the meaning or application of a statute.[37]

6. Interpretation of a Statute: The Plain Meaning Rule

When statutes are discussed in the case law, the primary focus is on what the statute says (or means) and on whether the law applies to the given situation.[38] It is universally agreed that the language of a statute is the starting point for its analysis.[39] The language of a statute, however, is not always clear on its face. Certain statutory language may be vague or may not address an issue arguably within the ambit of the law.

If the statutory language is unclear, a practitioner and courts would consider other cases in which this particular statute or statutes read in *pari materia*[40] have been construed. Existing case law that has interpreted a statute may be mandatory and, in any event, might be persuasive authority. It is also critical to review an agency's regulations and administrative adjudications. See Chapter IV.B. The legislative history of a particular statute may also shed light on the meaning of the law. See section that immediately follows.

7. Use of Legislative History

When neither the language of the statute, the regulations, nor the case law adequately addresses the issue at hand, the court may resort to legislative history to help resolve the dispute. Judges have a range of opinion on the utility of legislative history. Some judges reject altogether the use

---

[37] This, of course, is also true with respect to constitutional provisions. The sheer number of Supreme Court cases in which the due process clause of the 14th Amendment is interpreted and applied alone supports this proposition.

[38] Often, the first court called upon to analyze any given law will be asked to determine the constitutionality *vel non* of the law. Challenges to the constitutionality of a law are rarely successful.

[39] For a discussion of the *Chevron* doctrine, which controls the manner by which courts review statutory construction by administrative agencies, see Chapter VI.C.5.

[40] Statutes read in *pari materia* are statutes involving the same general subject matter and whose terms are to be read in a manner consistent with other, similarly worded statutes.

of legislative history as a tool of construction and rely exclusively on the language of the statute. Other judges believe that the legislative history is an appropriate tool for discerning the meaning, scope, and application of a statute.

Liberally construed, there are three phases of legislative history:

a. *Pre-enactment history:*

Policies and/or case law which prompted Congress to change the law. Pre-enactment history is considered to be a form of legislative history because it may help explain the reasons for congressional attention to the matter and specific changes achieved by Congress—either through modification of an existing statute or through enactment of a new statute to change the common law prospectively.

b. *Enactment history:*

The process by which a given bill becomes law, from introduction into Congress, through either signature by the U.S. President or congressional override of a Presidential veto. See Chapter III.D.

In connection with enactment history, committee reports are the most frequently cited documents of legislative history.

c. *Post-enactment history:*

Cases, administrative, and legislative treatment of a law after its enactment into law.

B.   Sources of Federal Statutory Law

There are three main sources of federal statutory law that are commonly used by students and practitioners. One is the official United States Code (U.S.C.). The others are commercial versions of the United States Code—the United States Code Annotated (U.S.C.A.) and the United States Code Service (U.S.C.S.).

All three versions contain the same Code. The U.S.C.A. and U.S.C.S. contain additional information about each section of the code, including case annotations. These, in turn, lead to cases in which those statutory provisions are discussed.* Whenever citing the Code, however, the official U.S.C. must be used—never cite to the U.S.C.A. or U.S.C.S.

---

* The U.S.C.S. and U.S.C.A. also contain case annotations relevant to each provision of the U.S. Constitution.

SOURCES OF STATUTORY LAW [Publisher]	CHARACTERISTICS	HOW TO LOCATE	UPDATING STATUTES
United States Code (U.S.C.) [Government Printing Office—Official Version]	Text of statute. Legislative annotations.	Index—By subject and name of act. Title Outline. 50 titles, separated into chapters and subchapters. Popular Name Index.	Annual Supplements. New Code issued every 6 years. Shepard's Citators for Statutes. Session Laws. Slip Laws.
United States Code Service (U.S.C.S.) [Lawyers' Cooperative]	Text of statute. Legislative annotations. Interpretive Notes and Decisions—Case annotations by subject, with index. References to A.L.R. and other sources. References to statutes that cite to this section. Aims to be selective, not comprehensive.	Index—By subject and name of act. Title Outline—50 titles, separated into chapters and subchapters. Popular Name Index.	Pocket Parts. Annual Supplements. Cumulative Later Case and Statutory Service—Cumulative; issued on a quarterly basis. U.S.C.S. Advance Sheets—Non-cumulative text; issued on a monthly basis. Shepard's Citators for Statutes.
United States Code Annotated (U.S.C.A.) [West]	Text of statute. Legislative annotations. Notes of Decisions—Case annotations by subject, with index. References to C.J.S. and other West resources.	Index—By subject and name of act. Title Outline—50 titles, separated into chapters and sub-chapters. Popular Name Index.	Pocket Parts. Annual Supplements. Advance pamphlets—Non-cumulative, issued about six times per year. U.S.C.C.A.N pamphlets—Non-cumulative text, monthly. Shepard's Citators for Statutes.
United States Code Congressional and Administrative News (U.S.C.C.A.N.)	Current congressional session's public laws. Chronological order. Not annotated. Also contains major congressional committee and sub-committee reports.	Public Law Number, in order of enactment.	Codification in the U.S.C.
Statutes at Large	Compendium of enacted laws that constitute official proof of enactment.	Public Law Number, in order of enactment.	Codification in U.S.C.
Session Laws	Compilation of slip laws from immediately preceding session.	Public Law Number, in order of enactment.	U.S.C.C.A.N.
Slip Laws	Copy of individual law in pamphlet form. First formal appearance of a newly-enacted law.	Public Law Number.	Session law compilation

C. Terminology Relating to Congressional Action

Congressional action has a language all its own. Set forth below is terminology peculiar to the legislative process and the meaning of those terms.

Amendment	Addition to bill or resolution; may be made at any time after introduction; often made to help forge compromise.
Bill	Proposed legislation introduced into either or both houses of Congress.
Chamber	Each "house" of Congress may also be referred to as a "chamber."
Codification	Process of adding laws into a code (for example, the United States Code, see Chapter III.B.).
Enabling Statutes	Statute that creates and empowers ("enables") an administrative agency to act. Also "implementing" statute.
Public Law	Chronological assignment of number to each law. Assigned when President signs a bill or when a presidential veto is overridden. Number comprised of year of congress and chronological number of bill, separated by hyphen.
Resolution	Congressional expression of opinion, thanks, censure, among other things. Not a law.
Rider	Specific type of amendment; generally attached to bill or resolution with the specific purpose of coercing opponents to favor passage of the bill or resolution.
Session Laws	Chronological compilation of all laws enacted by a legislature in a particular legislative session. Found in Statutes At Large. See Chapter III.B. Legal evidence of laws in all courts in U.S.—much of this has been codified. Not useful as research tool except insofar as a particular law has not yet been published in a code.
Slip Laws	First official form of publication of a federal law. Separately-paginated pamphlet text of each law. Designated by public law number. No index.

D. How a Bill Becomes a Law

The chart that follows discusses the process by which a proposed bill becomes law, and includes finding aids for sources with information about each of these stages of legislative action.

Stages of Passage of a Bill	Definitions/Further Explanation	Finding Tools
Introduction of a Bill	Draft law introduced by one or more members of Congress. Often, a bill will be introduced in both chambers simultaneously by respective sponsors in the House and Senate. Appropriations bills (*i.e.*, those involving spending of funds) technically must originate in the House of Representatives. Bill number is assigned, which reflects the chronological number of the bill, the house in which the bill is introduced, the number of the Congress, the session, and the year.	Congressional Record. CCH Congressional Index.
Committee/Subcommittee Assignments	Each bill is assigned to a relevant committee/subcommittee for consideration.	CCH Congressional Index.
Subcommittee Hearings/Reports	Testimony by various individuals. Reports/papers filed by Subcommittee upon request or unilaterally by interested persons/industries. Report issued by subcommittee on pending bill for consideration by committee and/or full chamber.	CIS Index and Abstracts. CCH Congressional Index. U.S.C.C.A.N.
Committee Hearings/Reports	Testimony by various individuals. Reports/papers filed by Committee upon request or unilaterally by interested persons/industries. Report issued by committee on pending bill for consideration by full chamber. [Note: Committee Reports are very important sources of legislative history.]	CIS Index and Abstracts. CQ Weekly Report. CCH Congressional Index. U.S.C.C.A.N.
Floor Debates/Report	Floor debates on bill in each chamber. Members may prepare and submit written statements.	Congressional Record.
Conference Report	Report of the Joint Committee resolving differences between House and Senate versions of a bill for presentation to full chamber of each house. [Note: Conference Reports are very important sources of legislative history.]	CIS Index and Abstract. U.S.C.C.A.N.
Chamber Votes	Each house votes on Conference version of bill. Simple majority of each house required to pass a bill. Votes of members of each house recorded.	Congressional Record. CCH Congressional Index.
Presentation to President	President may: • Sign bill into law; or • Veto bill; or • Do nothing—becomes law after 10 days, unless Congress has adjourned ("Pocket veto").	See Chapter IV.E. for sources of Presidential Documents.
Overriding a Veto	Two-thirds vote of *each* chamber required to override a presidential veto.	Congressional Record.

E. Legislative History: Finding Legislative History of a Federal Statute

The legislative history, as discussed above (see Chapter III.A.), traditionally describes the process through which legislation proceeds through Congress. The chart below describes the different publications and the legislative history events found in each of those publications.

Publication	Legislative History Materials Found in Publication
Congressional Record	Introduction of bills and resolutions. Text of some of the more important bills in original or amended form. Official voting record and vote tallies. Published daily while Congress in session. Text of floor debates. "Daily Digest" section includes summary of action in each house, dates of committee hearings, bills signed, committee hearings scheduled for the following day. "History of Bills and Resolutions" index published every two weeks. Cumulative Index.
Statutes at Large	Compilation of federal session laws, ordered by public law number. Index for acts contained in that volume only. Public law number may be gleaned from statutory references following each statutory section in U.S.C., U.S.C.A., and U.S.C.S. References to Congressional Record.
CCH Congressional Index	Digest of all public bills and resolutions. Status table reports action on bills and resolutions. Updated weekly while Congress is in session. Reports status of all pending legislation. Lists committee referrals. Records votes and indicates members who did not vote with the majority of their party. Measures enacted are indexed by public law number, bill number, sponsor, and subject.

United States Code Congressional and Administrative News (U.S.C.C.A.N.)	Text of public laws. Text of selected committee reports. Major legislative reports with related public law and some other relevant publications after passage of a law. Quick reference to legislative history—before text of each act, cross-reference to page on which legislative history appears. References to House and Senate reports.
CIS Abstract/Index	Abstracts and indexes documents comprising legislative history of statutes. Compilation of complete legislative history for every public law during each year. Includes hearing transcripts, reports, committee prints, references to Congressional Record, member voting records, status records. Two volumes for each Congress; monthly supplements; quarterly and annual cumulative index. Index of all bills introduced, by testimony, subject, sub-committee, title, bill number, report number, and document numbers, from 1970 to current year.
Digest of Public General Bills and Resolutions	Summaries of all bills and resolutions introduced in each session. Indices allow for retrieval by sponsor and cosponsor, short title, and subject.
Monthly Catalog of U.S. Government Publications	Listing and index to government publications.

CHAPTER IV

ADMINISTRATIVE AND OTHER EXECUTIVE LAW

A. Preliminary Points Relating to Federal Administrative Law

1. Federal Administrative Agencies are Authorized by Congress

Federal agencies exist by virtue of, and receive their authority to act from, statutes authorizing agency action enacted by the U.S. Congress. Statutes authorizing agency action are often vague and omit much of the detail necessary to be carried out effectively. Agencies, in turn, promulgate regulations, or rules of general applicability, which supplement or enhance the statutes and enable the agency to carry out those laws. Regulations are issued pursuant to public notice and comment procedures, as required by statute.[42]

2. Federal Administrative Agencies Regulate Diverse and Important Areas

Agencies cover a wide range of areas of federal law, and regulate areas as diverse as the transfer of securities, taxation, air travel, food and drugs, agriculture, and the national transportation and sale of various forms of energy.[43]

3. Federal Administrative Agency Action May Be "Legislative" or "Adjudicative"

Agencies engage in both quasi-legislative and quasi-judicial activities.

---

[42] The Administrative Procedure Act (APA), codified at various sections of Title 5 of the United States Code, requires among other things that agencies follow a particular set of procedures in issuing regulations.

[43] There are really two types of agencies—the administrative agencies that are created and empowered by Congress, and the semi-independent agencies that are part of the executive department. It is the former—the independent administrative agencies—that are the subject of this chapter.

Agencies perform quasi-legislative functions when they consider and issue rules and regulations designed to implement the legislation which they are charged with administering.

Agencies also engage in adjudications of live disputes between or among parties. The procedure followed in most agencies is as follows: An Administrative Law Judge (ALJ) will hold a trial-type hearing and make an initial merits disposition. This decision in most cases will be appealed to and reviewed by a higher agency body. Court review may follow. Given that there has been a thorough fact-finding and internal review process, court review of many agency actions begins in the court of appeals rather than in the district courts. See paragraph immediately below and Chapter VI.

4. Court Challenges to Agency Action

Challenges to federal agency actions are brought in federal court. Statutes governing court review of actions of many (but not all) agencies provide for judicial review in the United States Court of Appeals rather than in the United States District Court. These statutes are based on the premise that the agency has already served the fact-finding function that the district court would otherwise perform; accordingly, there is no reason for the district court to perform its traditional fact-finding process anew.

Challenges to agency action may take several forms.

Agency rules and regulations may be challenged at the time they are issued as arbitrary and capricious or otherwise contrary to law; they may be challenged for procedural irregularities; or they may be challenged as going beyond the agency's congressional mandate. Once a regulation is applied in a given case, challenges are confined to the application of that rule in that particular case.

Agency adjudications may also be challenged by parties aggrieved by an adjudication.

B. Agency Actions and Issuances[44]

The following chart depicts various agency issuances and the characteristics and purposes of each of those issuances, and presents the sources in which such issuances may be found.

It is of course imperative when doing research in the area of administrative law that case law (in particular federal cases when researching a matter of federal regulatory law) involving the relevant statutory scheme be consulted in addition to agency issuances.

---

[44] Agencies act pursuant to their enabling legislation. See Chapter III.C.

AGENCY ISSUANCE	PURPOSE/CHARACTERISTICS	HOW TO LOCATE
Adjudications	Agency in its "judicial" role. Resolution of actual disputes between live parties. Normally resolved in the first instance by an Administrative Law Judge (ALJ), with appeal to full agency.	Federal Register. See Chapter IV.D. Daily issuances by issuing agency (looseleaf services). [45]
Interpretative Guidelines/ Regulation Preambles	Generally accompany rulemakings. Agency statements about the newly-promulgated rule. Clarify and explain rules. Generally entitled to somewhat less weight than the regulations themselves.	Code of Federal Regulations. See Chapter IV.C. Federal Register. Daily issuances by issuing agency (looseleaf services).
Notices	Various types. Designed to put interested parties on notice of a filing by a regulated entity or action by the agency.	Federal Register. Daily issuances by issuing agency (looseleaf services).
Notice of Inquiry (NOI)	Precursor to "Notice of Proposed Rulemaking" (see below). Agency's initial, still tentative deliberation re: instituting a rulemaking on a specific subject. Calls for public comment.	Federal Register. Daily issuances by issuing agency (looseleaf services).
Notice of Proposed Rulemaking (NOPR)	Agency Notice that it is considering a rulemaking on a specific subject. Calls for public comment.	Federal Register. Daily issuances by issuing agency (looseleaf services).
Opinions	Usually refers to Administrative Law Judge determinations based on factual findings applied to the law.	Federal Register. Daily issuances by issuing agency (looseleaf services).
Orders	Final disposition of any agency proceeding other than a rulemaking.	Federal Register. Daily issuances by issuing agency (looseleaf services).
Policy Statements	Statements of agency expectation as to how it will rule in a given area or on a specific issue. Non-binding, and therefore not subject to judicial review.	Daily issuances by issuing agency (looseleaf services).
Rehearing/ Reconsideration	Agency evaluation of its earlier action at the request of one or more parties. Varies by agency, by statute and by rule—some agencies require rehearing/reconsideration. A party will not be able to seek judicial review if it does not follow the rehearing/reconsideration process.	Federal Register. Daily issuances by issuing agency (looseleaf services).
Rules And Regulations	Agency issuances of general applicability.	Code of Federal Regulations. Federal Register. Daily issuances by issuing agency (looseleaf services).

[45] Most agencies make available on a daily basis issuances that are either provided to practitioners before that agency and/or ultimately published in a commercial looseleaf service for that agency. See Chapter I.E.2.g.

C. The Code of Federal Regulations

The Code of Federal Regulations (C.F.R.) is a compilation of the rules and regulations of the federal agencies.

What Does the C.F.R. Contain?	Agency rules and regulations. See Chapter IV.B.
Relationship Between C.F.R. and Federal Register?	C.F.R. is the codification of portions of the Federal Register. See Chapter IV.D.
When Does the C.F.R. Issue?	Once per year; new color spine will indicate year.
How the C.F.R. Is Organized	50 Titles, divided by subject matter. Titles are divided into chapters, parts, and sections.
How to Use the C.F.R.	C.F.R. Index—by topic, agency, U.S.C. citation, Statutes at Large citation, Public Law number, and list of C.F.R. titles, chapters, sub-chapters, parts. Index updated two times per year to reflect changes to regulations as of January 1 and July 1. U.S.C.S. Index and Finding Aids to C.F.R.—by topic, U.S.C. citation, C.F.R. citation, statutes at large citation, list of C.F.R. titles, chapters, sub-chapters, and parts, agency, list of agency by C.F.R. title.
How to Update the C.F.R.	List of Sections Affected (L.S.A.)—Monthly compilation of changes to regulations, organized by C.F.R. title number, chapter, part, and section. Translates U.S.C. citation, Statutes at Large citation, and Executive Order number. Indicates where in Federal Register the changes are reflected. Shepard's Citators for federal regulations. See Chapter II.B.2. note 30.
Relationship Between C.F.R. and Statutes	C.F.R. contains the agency regulations that implement the legislation to which they relate. Title number of C.F.R. is often the same as the related statute, but this is not always the case.

How to Locate Cases Relevant to Agency Rules and Regulations	Check case annotations to authorizing[46] statute in U.S.C.A. or U.S.C.S. Consult looseleaf services (see Chapter I.E.2.g.) relating to that area of law. Shepardize the regulation. See Chapter II.B.2.

D. The Federal Register

The Federal Register is a daily publication of regulations, rules, notices, and other agency and official issuances. Certain documents published in the Federal Register become published, or "codified" in the Code of Federal Regulations. See Chapter IV.C.

What Does the Federal Register Contain?	Agency and other executive branch pronouncements: • The President—Executive Orders; Presidential Proclamations; Other Presidential Documents. • Federal Agencies—rules; regulations; general statements of policy; notice of proposed rulemakings; miscellaneous notices; etc. See C.F.R. Part 1.
When Does the Federal Register Issue?	Daily.
How to Use the Federal Register	Daily list of parts of C.F.R. affected by C.F.R. title number and part number. Monthly list of sections affected. December index; or latest month's index plus daily issuances since the end of that month. Subject indices—cumulative; updated annually.
How to Update the Federal Register	List of C.F.R. Sections Affected, by cumulative monthly supplement. Daily lists of C.F.R. Parts Affected since most recent monthly supplement. December index, cumulative for year.
Relationship Between Federal Register and C.F.R.	Federal Register can be viewed as the "pocket part" or daily supplement to the C.F.R. (including List of Sections Affected). Rules and regulations ultimately get "codified" in the C.F.R.

---

[46] An authorizing statute is the same as an implementing or enabling statute. See Chapter III.C.

E. Presidential Documents

Types of Presidential Document	Description of Document
Executive Orders	Have force and effect of law. Usually issued pursuant to specific statutory authority. May also be issued pursuant to constitutional authority. May not legislate or override congressional action.
Presidential Proclamations	"Softer" presidential statements. Often involve "housekeeping" matters or may commemorate person, place, or event.
Presidential Legislative Statements	Presidential statements accompanying signing or vetoing of legislation.

Sources for Presidential Documents:

1. Federal Register
2. Weekly Compilation of Presidential Documents
3. Title 3 of the Code of Federal Regulations
4. Statutes at Large
5. U.S.C.C.A.N.
6. Federal Index
7. Congressional Information Service Abstracts*
8. CQ Weekly*
9. CQ Almanac*
10. CQ Weekly Report*
11. Congressional Record*
12. CCH Congressional Index*

*Presidential documents specifically relating to legislation—passed and pending—are indicated by an asterisk. The other sources listed may include presidential legislative statements, but will also include presidential statements of other types.

CHAPTER V

CIVIL LITIGATION

A. Preliminary Points Relating to the Federal Civil Litigation Process

The discussion that follows covers issues of federal litigation and the citations, accordingly, are to federal authorities. Civil litigation in most states is similar to the federal paradigm, but differences do exist. It is thus vital that one look to state law for state law issues, rules, and procedures.

1. Civil Litigation Defined

Civil litigation involves disputes between or among parties over virtually any matter that is not governed by an administrative body.

Civil litigation is also to be distinguished from criminal litigation. Criminal cases at the federal level are governed primarily by the Federal Rules of Criminal Procedure, and also implicate a number of important constitutional protections and issues which will not be addressed here.

2. The Importance of Issues Relating to Jurisdiction and Venue

Issues relating to jurisdiction and venue must always be considered before instituting a lawsuit. A defendant may challenge the plaintiff's choice of jurisdiction and venue. In addition, the court *sua sponte* (on its own motion) may challenge its jurisdiction to hear a case.

Jurisdiction in this context refers to the type of court which will have jurisdiction to review the action at hand.* For instance, is there federal court jurisdiction over the dispute presented? Or is jurisdiction in the state courts? Is there jurisdiction in *both* the state and federal courts?

Venue refers to the *place* in which a case will be brought. For instance, if it is determined that there is federal court jurisdiction, it still must be determined in which district court the case should be brought.

Jurisdiction and venue at the federal level are governed by various provisions of Title 28 of the United States Code, and by agency-specific statutes.

---

* There is also the question whether the court has *personal* jurisdiction over the defendant. Unlike court jurisdiction over the matter presented, objections to personal jurisdiction may be waived.

3. Issues of Timing

The time by which certain actions and events must take place are of extreme importance in federal civil litigation. For instance, certain objections not raised by a particular time in the proceeding are deemed to have been waived. The Federal Rules of Civil Procedure set forth the timetable by which certain events must take place. Dates established by court order, of course, must also be adhered to.

4. Researching Federal Rules of Civil Procedure

Methods for researching case law involving the meaning and application of the Federal Rules of Civil Procedure include the U.S.C.A. (under Title 28) and the U.S.C.S. (under Rules). There are also several definitive treatises and other services that discuss the application of the Federal Rules of Civil Procedure.

B. Civil Litigation Process

The following chart describes the typical civil litigation process in federal court (*i.e.,* in a United States District Court). The approach followed in many states pursuant to state court rules is similar.

Local court rules should *always* be consulted by the practitioner at every juncture in the procedure.

Complaint [Fed. R. Civ. Proc. 7, 8][47]	Filed by plaintiff to commence lawsuit. Identifies parties, establishes jurisdiction and venue. Identifies cause(s) of action. Requests specific relief. Modern notice pleading does not require that counsel set forth elaborate facts or grounds for relief. However, failure to investigate to ensure that the bringing of a lawsuit is not frivolous may lead to sanctions being imposed upon the attorney or the party (if *pro se*)[48] pursuant to Rule 11 of the Federal Rules of Civil Procedure.[49]

---

[47] The Federal Rules of Civil Procedure is the most important body of rules applicable to civil litigation at the federal level. The Federal Rules of Evidence and the local rules of each particular district court are also exceedingly important to the federal civil litigation process.

[48] A *pro se* party is one who proceeds without an attorney.

[49] Rule 11 of the Federal Rules of Civil Procedure is applicable to all papers filed, not just the complaint. Sanctions may also be applied in federal appellate courts. See Chapter VI.B. note 58.

Summons [Fed. R. Civ. Proc. 55]	Order by the court clerk made upon the filing of the complaint. Requires response by defendant.
Service [Fed. R. Civ. Proc. 4(d)]	Complaint and summons must be delivered to other party or parties to lawsuit.[50]
Answer [Fed. R. Civ. Proc. 7, 8]	Filed by defendant in response to complaint. Responds in order to each allegation in complaint. Must include all affirmative defenses (*e.g.*, statute of limitations, lack of personal jurisdiction). May include counterclaim and/or cross-claim. The defendant may file a motion to dismiss in lieu of a traditional answer.
Reply [Fed. R. Civ. Proc. 7, 8]	Reply is required if the answer contains a counterclaim. Reply may also be made by plaintiff with permission of the court.
Counterclaim [Fed. R. Civ. Proc. 13]	Claim by any party against an opposing party (*e.g.*, defendant versus plaintiff). May be "compulsory" (arising out of same transaction or occurrence—must be made or waived) or "permissive" (may be made at some later time).
Cross-Claim [Fed. R. Civ. Proc. 13(g)]	Claim by one party against a co-party (*e.g.*, one defendant against another defendant) arising out of the same transaction or subject matter of the original action or any counterclaim thereto.
Intervention [Fed. R. Civ. Proc. 24]	Process by which interested person not named in lawsuit seeks court order allowing its participation. Normally, intervenors may not introduce into the proceedings issues not raised by the principal parties.

---

[50] Indeed, all documents provided to the court must be "served" upon the other parties to the lawsuit. In order to establish that service has been accomplished according to the rules, the serving party must provide a "certificate of service" in which the fact and manner of service are identified. Failure to make service as required by the rules could result in the appearance of an *ex parte* (*i.e.*, one-sided) communication between the judge and the party filing the papers in question. The court as a result may order that the filing be stricken from the record.

Motion[51] to Dismiss [Fed. R. Civ. Proc. 12(b)]	Several grounds upon which dismissal may be had: • Lack of subject-matter jurisdiction; • Lack of personal jurisdiction; • Improper venue; • Insufficiency of process; • Insufficiency of service of process; • Failure to state a claim upon which relief can be granted; • Failure to join a necessary party. Most important/widely used are: • Motion to Dismiss for Lack of Subject Matter Jurisdiction (Rule 12(b)(1)); and • Motion to Dismiss for Failure to State Claim Upon Which Relief Can Be Granted (Rule 12(b)(6)). Motion to Dismiss for Lack of Subject Matter Jurisdiction: • May be raised at any time; • Affects the jurisdiction of the court and cannot be waived; • May be raised *sua sponte* by the court (*i.e.,* on the court's own motion). Motion to Dismiss for Failure to State a Claim Upon Which Relief Can Be Granted: • Even if all facts pleaded are true, there is no cause of action;[52] • May be filed by any party against whom a claim has been filed (defendant, counter-claimant, cross-claimant); • If granted, case is over; moving party wins on the merits.

---

[51] The party filing any motion is referred to as the "movant." The party opposing a motion is referred to as the "non-moving party," the "respondent," or the "opponent" to the motion.

[52] The term "demurrer" is largely an obsolete term (still used in some jurisdictions) to refer to a process similar to a motion to dismiss for failure to state a cause of action on which relief can be granted.

Discovery [Fed. R. Civ. Proc. 26-37] See Chapter V.C.	Fact-gathering process. Engaged in by all parties. Several forms: • Written interrogatories; • Requests for production of documents and things; • Requests for admission; • Oral deposition; • Medical examination (physical or mental) upon motion and showing of good cause; • Automatic disclosure required of certain basic information and documents pertaining to the case; no request need be made. Discovery may be had of a party's expert witnesses if those witnesses are expected to testify at trial. It is difficult to get discovery about experts who are not expected to testify at trial.
Motion for Summary Judgment [Fed. R. Civ. Proc. 56]	Motion to dismiss case for alleged lack of genuine facts sufficient for jury to find in favor of non-movant; the facts are not in dispute and therefore there is no reason for the court to waste the resources of the jury. Theory: No reasonable jury could find for opposing (non-moving) party. Facts are so clear that allowing the judge to usurp the fact-finding role of the jury is not inconsistent with the jury's function. May be filed by either party. May be full, relating to entire case; or partial, relating to some portion of the case. If moving party wins complete motion for summary judgment, the case is over in favor of the moving party.
Other Pre-Trial Motions [Fed. R. Civ. Proc. 7(b)]	May relate to discovery, admissibility of evidence, etc. Often called a motion *in limine*.[53] Generally, any party can file a motion at any time to seek a court order.

---

[53] A motion *in limine* is a pre-trial motion requesting that the court prohibit opposing counsel from referring to or offering up evidence on matters considered to be so highly prejudicial to the moving party that the moving party wants to avoid any exposure of that evidence to the jury.

Other Pre-Trial Motions *(cont'd)*	Parties are expected to attempt to resolve their differences before seeking court intervention. Parties seeking relief file a *motion;* parties answering the motion file a *response* or an *answer.*
Settlement/Status Conferences [Fed. R. Civ. Proc. 16]	Efforts at informal dispute resolution. May be ordered/scheduled by the court. Judge may be present. Discovery may help the parties analyze the relative strength of their cases, which may ultimately assist in the development of a settlement.
Voir Dire [Fed. R. Civ. Proc. 47]	Questioning/selection of prospective jurors. Questioning may be by counsel or judge. Counsel may challenge a juror "for cause" (*e.g.,* juror knows a party), or under a "peremptory challenge," under which counsel need not specify the nature of the objection. Objections, however, may not be based on race or gender.[54]
Trial [Fed. R. Civ. Proc. 38-53]	Presentation of evidence to finder of fact. Includes testimony, documentary evidence, illustrative evidence. Evidence presented first by plaintiff, then by defendant, with a rebuttal by plaintiff. Witnesses subject to direct examination by the party sponsoring witness; then subject to cross-examination by opposing party; opportunity for re-direct examination by party sponsoring the witness; and finally re-cross by the opposing party. Framed on either side by counsels' opening statements and closing arguments. Most trials are heard by a jury as fact-finder; sometimes, if the parties agree, the judge will be the finder of fact. This is called a "bench trial."

---

[54] Another type of *voir dire* is questioning by counsel during the course of the trial out of the hearing of the jury.

Judgment as a Matter of Law [Fed. R. Civ. Proc. 50]	Judgment granted to moving party on the grounds that there is no legally sufficient evidence for a reasonable jury to find for the non-moving party. Motion may be made by either party at end of trial for the court to order a verdict in its favor, and *again* after the verdict is rendered. Very rarely granted. Results in a finding that the jury verdict lacked sufficient legal basis. If successful, moving party wins case. Replaces in part former Judgment Notwithstanding the Verdict.
Jury Charge [Fed. R. Civ. Proc. 51]	Instructions by court to guide jury deliberations. Judge presents the law which the jury is to apply to the facts. In advance of jury charge, parties submit proposed instructions; may be contentious process.
Verdict	Jury decision based on its application of law as charged to facts as presented at trial, as interpreted by jury.
Appeals [Fed. R. Civ. Proc. 77-80]	Aggrieved party may seek appeal to higher level court. Appeals based on alleged error of law—appeals courts will not review factual issues. Statutes and court rules govern the taking of appeals.

C. Summary of Discovery Process

Discovery, it is recalled (see Chapter V.B.), is the fact-finding process engaged in by the parties in anticipation of trial, summary judgment motions, and/or settlement negotiations. The following chart outlines the major forms of discovery endorsed by the Federal Rules of Civil Procedure.

Forms of Discovery[55]	*Written Interrogatories—Fed. R. Civ. Proc. 33:* Written questions seeking written responses. *Requests for the Production of Documents and Things—Fed. R. Civ. Proc. 34:* Written request to produce documents and other items related to the litigation. Response is usually an invitation to review documents to be made available by responding party. *Requests to Admit—Fed. R. Civ. Proc. 36:* Written allegations to which recipient is to admit or deny, in writing. Failure to do so by prescribed time will result in allegations being "deemed admitted." Cost of proving allegations not admitted but which should have been falls on recipient. *Oral Depositions—Fed. R. Civ. Proc. Rule 30:* Verbal answers given under oath to oral questions.
When Discovery Occurs	Right to discovery attaches upon filing of lawsuit. Discovery often lasts for years and delays trial date or other merits disposition accordingly. Discovery often has the salutary purpose of allowing the parties to assess more accurately their settlement strategies. Courts often impose deadlines by which discovery shall have taken place.
Discovery From Third Persons	Discovery may be compelled of a person not party to the lawsuit through a subpoena [Fed. R. Civ. Proc. 45]. Third persons may be required to produce documents and other physical evidence; to provide deposition testimony; and to provide testimony at trial.

---

[55] As noted in Chapter V.B., there are other forms of discovery available under the Federal Rules of Civil Procedure.

Common Discovery-Related Motions	*Motions to Compel Discovery—Fed. R. Civ. Proc. 37(a):* Request that court order recipient of discovery request to provide answer to same. *Motion for Protective Order—Fed. R. Civ. Proc. 26(c):* Request that court not require response by recipient of discovery request. Grounds may include that the requests are overbroad (*i.e.,* that requesting party is engaging in a "fishing expedition"), irrelevant, or that disclosure would violate the attorney-client privilege or would require the disclosure of attorney work-product.[56] Courts generally look with extreme displeasure on the filing of motions for protective orders and motions to compel discovery. The parties are expected to make every effort to resolve discovery conflicts on their own before resorting to court intervention.

---

[56] Generally speaking, the attorney-client privilege protects from disclosure to opposing counsel communications between a lawyer and client. The work product immunity doctrine gives *qualified* immunity to most writings made by an attorney about a matter in anticipation of litigation, and absolute immunity to the attorney's mental impressions, legal theories, etc.

CHAPTER VI

APPELLATE COURT REVIEW

A. Preliminary Points Relating to Federal Appellate Court Review

1. Decisions Reviewed

The Court of Appeals generally reviews decisions of district courts and of federal agencies. The decisions of many federal agencies are reviewed in the first instance in the Court of Appeals under the theory that the agency below has served the fact-finding process normally reserved for the district court.

2. Appeals versus Petitions for Review

a. Appeals   Appeals are objections taken from district court decisions.

The primary parties to an appeal are the "appellant" (the party taking appeal and seeking review of the lower court decision) and the "appellee" (the party supporting the lower court's determination and defending the appeal).

b. Petitions for Review   Petitions for review are objections taken by parties aggrieved by an agency order.

The primary parties to a petition for review are the "petitioner" and the "respondent." In these cases, the agency (and sometimes the United States) will be the respondent, seeking to uphold its order.

3. Function of Appellate Court Review

The function of appellate court review is to identify and correct errors of law below (*e.g.,* by the district court or the agency whose determinations are under review by the appeals court).

Appellate courts review issues of law, not fact. The appellate court may reverse or remand incorrect district court or agency determinations of fact if they are so egregious as to amount to an abuse of discretion.

4. Remedial Options for Reviewing Court

An appeals court has broad latitude in resolving appeals or petitions for review.

Among the options available to it, the appeals court may affirm the determination under review; it may reverse the determination under review; or it may remand the underlying decision for further action consistent with the appeals court's determination. See Chapter VIII.B.3.

When the court of appeals intends to compel a particular result, its normal procedure would be to remand to the district court or agency with an order that it enter the prescribed outcome or relief.[57]

5. Issues of Timing

Issues of timing are extremely important in the appellate process. For instance, failure to follow statutory time limits for filing a notice of appeal or petition for review will result in a loss of appellate jurisdiction and the aggrieved party will not be able to pursue appellate court review.

6. Researching Federal Rules of Appellate Procedure

Methods for researching case law involving the meaning and application of the Federal Rules of Appellate Procedure include the U.S.C.A. (under Title 28) and the U.S.C.S. (under Rules).

There are also any number of definitive treatises and other commercial services that discuss the Federal Rules of Appellate Procedure.

B.   Federal Appellate Litigation Process[58]

The following chart represents the basic process of taking an appeal in a federal court (*i.e.*, the United States Court of Appeals) from a district court opinion or of petitioning for review of an agency action. As always, local appellate court rules should be consulted by the practitioner.

State court rules may provide for similar procedures in state appeals courts.

---

[57] Given separation of powers concerns, it is far more likely that an appeals court would order a particular result on review of a district court decision than of an agency order. See Chapter VI.C.5.

[58] Sanctions may be imposed on practitioners before the federal court of appeals. See Federal Rule of Appellate Procedure 38; 28 U.S.C. § 1927 (1994).

Notice of Appeal or Petition for Review [Fed. R. App. Proc. 3, 15]	Mechanism by which appealing/petitioning parties notify court and opposing party of intent to appeal lower court or agency determination.[60]
Interventions [Fed. R. App. Proc. 15(d)]	Process by which interested persons that are not direct parties in the appeal/review proceeding seek court order allowing their participation.[61] Normally, intervenors may not introduce into the proceedings issues not raised by the principal parties.
Docketing Statements and Other Court Filing Requirements [Fed. R. App. Proc. 12]	Court requirements that parties submit information about the case, related cases, the parties' corporate affiliations, and other related information.
Motions [Fed. R. App. Proc. 27]	Requests for relief of any type may be filed by any party (or non-party, in the case of requests for intervention or *amici* participation (see Chapter VII.)), at any time in the proceeding.
Dispositive/Calendaring Motions	Motions that may affect the disposition or calendaring of the case (such as motions to hold in abeyance, to withdraw appeal, to grant summary affirmance). Such motions should be made as soon as practicable. Court rule may impose deadline.
Briefing Schedule [Fed. R. App. Proc. 28, Briefing, generally]	Court-imposed briefing schedule. Court may solicit suggestions from the parties.
Record [Fed. R. App. Proc. 10-11, 16-17]	The record consists of the contents of the proceedings of the district court or the agency. This will include all filings by all parties, all transcripts and other pieces of evidence, all court or agency pronouncements, and anything else that was before the court or agency in making its decision that is the subject of appellate court review. The appellate court's review will be limited to the contents of the "record."

---

60 The time for taking appeal or seeking a petition for review will differ depending upon the type of decision from which appellate review is sought.

61 Intervenors may participate in either type of appellate court review. In petitions for review, intervenors on the side of the agency may well be the real parties in interest, since they do not have the option of being named respondent.

Petitioner's/Appellant's Opening Brief [Fed. R. App. Proc. 28(a)]	Brief on the merits, devoted to showing legal error in the disposition below and reasons why the lower court or agency determination should not be upheld.
Respondent's/Appellee's Responsive Brief [Fed. R. App. Proc. 28(b)]	Response to opening brief, arguing that lower court or agency decision should be affirmed.
Petitioner's/Appellant's Reply Brief [Fed. R. App. Proc. 28(c)]	Opportunity for petitioner/appellant to reply to arguments raised in respondent's/appellee's brief.
Oral Argument [Fed. R. App. Proc. 34]	Responsive argument between petitioners/ appellants and respondents/appellees. Judges on panel typically interject questions for the litigants. Courts in few but increasing number of cases may decide case without oral argument on the merits of the briefs, based on panel decision that oral argument would not be necessary.
Decision/ Entry of Judgment [Fed. R. App. Proc. 36]	Court's decision will usually be issued some time after oral argument (this is taking the case "under advisement"). On appeal, court will review issues of law *de novo,* and will not affirm lower court decision unless it independently concludes that district court made the correct rulings.[62]
Petition for Reconsideration or Suggestion for Rehearing En Banc [Fed. R. App. Proc. 35, 40]	Petition for Reconsideration asks the panel on the case to reconsider its ruling. Suggestion for Rehearing *En Banc* is a request that the entire court sit together to consider the panel's determination. [Note: The *en banc* procedure is rarely granted, but is vital in certain cases, given the general principle that decisions of one panel cannot be overturned by another panel but only by the entire court sitting *en banc.* See Chapters I.F.4. and II.G.3.b.]

---

[62] But see discussion of appellate court review of agency actions in which the courts defer to reasonable agency interpretations of statutes. See Chapter VI.C.5.

Mandate [Fed. R. App. Proc. 41]	21 days after an appellate court issues its decision in a case, a "mandate" issues, which is the formal order of the court. Issuance of the mandate will be delayed in the event of the filing of a petition for rehearing or a petition for a writ of *certiorari*. See Chapters I.H.3.a. and VIII.B.4.
Supreme Court Review [Part III. and Part IV. of the Rules of the Supreme Court]	Parties may seek appeal to Supreme Court in limited cases (see Chapter I.H.3.a.); or Parties may seek discretionary Court review through a petition for a writ of *certiorari*.

C. Special Issues Involving Appellate Court Review of Agency Action

As indicated above, the final orders of many federal agencies are appealed directly to the United States Court of Appeals. There are several issues specific to this context that should be emphasized.

1. Threshold Issues

Threshold issues of standing, finality, ripeness, and mootness may play a particularly significant role in these cases. See Chapter I.C.1.

2. Issues of Jurisdiction and Venue

When seeking appellate court review of final agency action, the practitioner should be careful to consider the unique rules relating to jurisdiction and venue that might be applicable.

3. Specific Federal Rules of Appellate Procedure Applicable to Agency Review Proceedings

The Federal Rules of Appellate Procedure contain specific rules applicable only to agency review proceedings. See Title IV of the Federal Rules of Appellate Procedure, Rules 15-20. Most local circuit court rules also have special provisions for the execution of petitions for review of agency determinations.

4. Importance of Administrative Procedure Act and Other Statutes

Agency actions, including, to some extent, the nature and scope of appellate review, are governed by the Administrative Procedure Act

("APA"), codified at various sections of Title 5 of the United States Code; and other statutes applicable to particular agencies.

5. Court Deference to Agency Actions

Agencies act pursuant to congressional authorization and delegation of authority. For this reason, courts are particularly loathe to disrupt agency determinations, as review of agency orders raises concerns for the appropriate sphere of judicial review and separation of powers. Thus, in petitions for review even more than in appeals from district court determinations, the appeals courts are likely to give broad discretion to the agency to act pursuant to its delegated authority as it sees fit. For instance, the so-called *Chevron** doctrine requires that a court uphold an agency construction of a statute it is charged with administering as long as the agency's construction of that statute is "reasonable" and not inconsistent with the language of the act.

The court's analysis under *Chevron* is a two-step process:

1. Does the statute have a plain meaning? If the statute has a plain meaning, that meaning will control its application.
2. If the statute's meaning is not clear on its face, the agency's interpretation will be upheld if it is "reasonable."

In undertaking its *Chevron* analysis, the court will consult other cases involving the same or related statutes.

This, of course, is not to say that agencies are given anything approaching carte blanche. To the contrary, the judicial review function in the context of final agency determinations has always been considered extremely critical. Indeed, there are several judicial doctrines that preserve the importance of court review of agency actions. For instance, under the so-called *Chenery*** doctrine, the agency must have stated in the order under review the reasons for its action; post hoc rationales advanced by counsel or thought up by the court will not suffice to uphold an agency decision. In addition, a presumption of reviewability attaches to most final agency actions.

Because of the sensitive nature of the relationship between federal agencies and the federal courts, the courts are disinclined to order outright reversal of agency action. If the court finds that the agency has not adequately supported its actions or otherwise has not acted in a manner consistent with the law, the court will normally remand the case to the agency for reconsideration and further action.

---

*   *Chevron, U.S.A., Inc. v. Natural Resources Defense Council, Inc.,* 467 U.S. 837 (1984).

** *SEC v. Chenery Corp.,* 332 U.S. 194 (1947).

CHAPTER VII

OVERVIEW OF PARTY DESIGNATIONS AND THEIR ROLES IN THE CIVIL LITIGATION PROCESS

There are a number of parties that participate in the civil litigation process, each having a different role.

In this context, it should be noted that the term "civil litigation process" refers to all levels of court intervention—from the trial court level, to intermediate or appellate review, through supreme or high court judgment.

This chart shows the designations of the parties and defines their role at each court level.

Level of Proceeding	Party Designation	Role in the Process
Trial Court Level	Plaintiff[63]	Party bringing action for relief.
	Defendant[64]	Party against whom action is brought.
	Counterclaimant	Defendant in posture of bringing counterclaim against plaintiff.
	Cross-claimant	Defendant in posture of bringing claim against third party as responsible for any damages owed to plaintiff.
	Third-party defendant	Party in posture of defending against cross-claim for any damages owed to plaintiff.
	Intervenor	Interested party participating in litigation upon permission of the court.

---

[63] "Plaintiff" is often designated in shorthand as "P" or Π.

[64] "Defendant" is often designated in shorthand as "D" or Δ.

Appellate Court Level	Appellant	Unsuccessful party below, bringing appeal.
	Appellee	Party defending outcome below.
	Petitioner	Party challenging action below, usually in agency context.
	Respondent	Party defending action below, usually agency.
	Intervenor	Same as intervenor in trial court.
	Amicus curiae	"Friend of the court." Not really a party, but given leave (*i.e.*, permission) by the court to participate.
	U.S. Solicitor	Attorney for the U.S.; may participate in cases of great importance.
Supreme Court Level	Petitioner	Party seeking Supreme Court review and, if granted, urging rejection of the court's decision below.
	Respondent	Party opposing Supreme Court review and, if granted, defending resolution of the decision below.
	Intervenor	Same as intervenor in trial/appeals court.
	Amicus curiae	Same as *amicus curiae* in appeals court.
	U.S. Solicitor	Attorney for U.S.; may participate in *certiorari* practice, briefing, and argument.

CHAPTER VIII

OVERVIEW OF COURT ISSUANCES AND DISPOSITIONS

A. Sources of Court Issuances

Most appellate and high court decisions of substance at both the federal and state levels are published.[65]

Once an opinion is issued by a court, there is some lag time before the decision will actually appear in a reporter. Nevertheless, there are other sources by which a practitioner can access a court's decision. The table below demonstrates, in the order available, the forms of court issuances that are generally available.[66]

It is generally within the discretion of the issuing court as to whether an opinion of the court will or will not get published.

Some courts issue decisions which are designated by local rule as "not published" and therefore not suitable to be used as precedent. Practitioners, however, tend to cite to and rely upon even unpublished opinions that are so designated.

Court Issuance	Description
Slip Opinions	Paper issuances provided to parties soon after issuance by court. Limited copies may be available to the press and the public.
Memorandum Orders/Opinions	Also in "slip," or paper form. Short orders that generally will not be published. Often embody the court's ruling on a motion or appeal, with only a brief explanation.

---

[65] To be published means to appear in a printed reporter. Because most trial court decisions are jury verdicts, relatively few trial court opinions are published.

[66] The Office of the Clerk of the issuing court will often provide slip opinions or other paper forms of a court opinion upon request and for a nominal or per page fee. Many opinions—both published and unpublished—are also available through computerized legal research databases.

Advance Sheets	Initial printed version of the court's reported opinion. Paperback form, later incorporated into bound reporters.
Reporters	Bound, final version of the reported court's opinion.

B. Court Dispositions

1. General Court Dispositions

Order*	Court resolution of a motion. Court may grant a motion, deny a motion, or grant or deny a motion in part. May also be part of court's "ordering paragraph," which sets out the court's judgment and any requirements it is imposing on the parties or lower tribunals. Court may issue an order *sua sponte*.
Opinion	Reasoning and decision of the court. Court's application of law to facts. Includes statement of relevant controlling authority. Explanation of underlying principles and reasoning governing court's decision.
Judgment	Narrow disposition of the case. Generally found at end of opinion.
Holding	That portion of the opinion that answers the legal question raised by the facts of the controversy before it. See Chapter II.C.
Decision	Less precise term that may refer to the judgment, opinion, or holding of the court.
Dicta	That portion of a court's reasoning which is not necessary for the holding. Not controlling for future cases, but parties often rely on it as having some persuasive effect or other legal status that should be applied in subsequent cases. See Chapter II.C.
Decree	Obsolete term. "Judgment" is currently used in lieu of "decree."
Denial	Refusal to order relief requested in a motion.

---

* A court *order* is differentiated from a court *rule* in that an order is particular to a set of facts and circumstances before the court and is applicable to the litigants in that case. A rule is more generally applicable to parties before the court.

2. Dispositions Peculiar to Trial Court Practice

Injunction; Preliminary Injunction; Temporary Restraining Order	Court order that a person refrain from taking certain action. Preliminary injunction may be ordered in advance of a merits review, which may be a "temporary restraining order" (requested and granted very early in the process) or a "preliminary injunction" (granted before a merits review but not as immediate as a temporary restraining order). Moving party has the burden to show the need for the restraining order, including the immediate likelihood of irreparable harm in the absence of the injunction.
Interlocutory Ruling	Ruling which may be appealed in advance of the termination of the proceeding.[67] Relatively few rulings are subject to interlocutory review.
Judgment as a Matter of Law	Request by either party that the court grant a verdict in its favor, made at the end of trial. Judge may grant a directed verdict when the evidence is so strong in favor of the moving party that a reasonable jury could not find for the other party. Judge must consider all of the evidence in light most favorable to the non-moving party. Very rarely granted.

3. Dispositions Peculiar to Appellate Practice[68]

Affirmance	Court upholds the decision below (that is, of the lower court or agency decision on appeal).
Reversal	Rejection of holding of lower court or agency order.
Remand	Return of case to the lower court or agency for further factual findings or for other resolution consistent with appellate decision.
Vacatur	Court rejection of underlying decision in which the underlying decision is set aside and becomes void and without effect. Usually accompanied by a remand.
Modify	Court upholds part of lower tribunal's decision, but modifies it to be consistent with the law as determined by the appeals court.

---

67 As this suggests, most rulings may not be appealed to a higher court until the case is decided in full. Interlocutory rulings, for example grant of summary judgment, are the exception to this general principle.

68 Most of the dispositions listed as peculiar to appellate practice also apply to Supreme Court practice.

Mandate	Official manner by which court's opinion is issued and takes on the force and effect of law. Order of court directing lower tribunal to take specific action or make specified disposition.
Opinion of the Court	Opinion of the majority of the court.
Concurring Opinion	Separate opinion agreeing with the court's holding, but either disagreeing with the court's rationale or adding a rationale.
Dissenting Opinion	Separate opinion disagreeing with the court's holding.
Per Curiam *Opinion*	"By the court;" usually a brief announcement of the disposition without a written opinion.
Opinion on Rehearing	Opinion of initial merits panel on rehearing at request of one or more parties to the case. Rehearing is often requested but rarely granted.
En Banc *Opinion*	Opinion of all members of the court rather than a panel of judges sitting together to hear a particular case. *En banc* opinions are somewhat rare and are usually reserved for issues of extreme importance or to overrule (reject) an earlier court precedent. [Based on the theory that only the court sitting *en banc* can overrule a decision of a panel.]

4. Dispositions Peculiar to Supreme Court Practice

Plurality Opinion	Opinion which more justices sign than do any one concurring opinion, but which does not constitute a majority of the Court and hence does not have the force of precedent.
Summary Dispositions	*Per curiam* or memorandum decisions on the merits. Court does not reveal reasons for disposition, or only scant reasoning supplied. Constitutes a merits decision by the Court.
Certiorari *Granted*	Grant of discretionary review by the United States Supreme Court. Not a decision on the merits; does not reverse or otherwise directly affect lower court judgment.

Certiorari *Granted* (cont'd)	As a practical matter, may undermine strength of lower court ruling until the Supreme Court resolves issue.
Certiorari *Denied*	Refusal of the United States Supreme Court to entertain discretionary review of lower court decision. Not a decision on the merits; should not be construed as having any precedential effect.

CHAPTER IX

BASIC LEGAL CITATION FORM–
AN OVERVIEW

A. The *Bluebook*[69] Generally

The *Bluebook* provides the citation convention for American legal documents. The *Bluebook* has a dual focus: it is intended for law reviews/legal scholarship and for law practitioners (the focus here).

It is of critical importance that the law practitioner use the *Bluebook* correctly and accurately. There are at least three reasons why the practitioner must be meticulous about following the *Bluebook* protocol:

1. *Provides important information about a cited authority:* The citation form prescribed in the *Bluebook* imparts important information to the reader about the cited authority (year, jurisdiction, etc.).

2. *Allows reader to locate cited authority:* The citation form prescribed by the *Bluebook* provides information to allow the reader to locate the authority cited.

3. *Establishes writer's credibility:* The incorrect use of citations will result in a loss of credibility with the reader. The use of proper citation form, among other things, reflects appropriate attention to detail.

As noted, The *Bluebook* is intended both for practitioners and for legal scholarship. The practitioner can easily access the rules applicable to practice by using the back inside cover of the *Bluebook* and by reading the Practitioners' Notes, which is the first set of blue pages towards the front of the *Bluebook* (P.1-P.7).

The *Bluebook* also contains a comprehensive index which allows the user to access virtually any point regarding proper citation form.

---

[69] A *Uniform System of Citation* provides the standard reference for citations in American legal documents, and is more commonly referred to as "the *Bluebook*."

When using the *Bluebook,* keep in mind the credo that "Every character and every space begs a question." Proper *Bluebook* form imposes rules that are so specific they cover spacing, punctuation, capitalization, underlining/italicization, and the like.

B. General Rules of Style

Jump/Pinpoint Citations	Pages in cited source standing for specific proposition cited. Always use when quoting language. Almost always use in all other situations.
Citation Sentences/ Citation Clauses	Citation *sentences* begin and end with a period and appear at the end of a sentence of text. Citation *clauses* are set off by commas and appear somewhere in the middle of a sentence of text.
Introductory Signals	Indicate the relationship between the authority cited and the proposition for which it is cited. The closer the relationship between the cited authority and the proposition for which cited, the more direct a signal you will use. Introductory signals are almost always used with case citations, unless you are *quoting* from the authority cited. No signal is to be used when quoting from authority. Signals are set out in the *Bluebook* Rule 1.2.
Parentheticals	Used to indicate some detail about the proposition for which source is being cited. Strongly recommended where an introductory signal has been used. May also indicate some important information about the decision (*e.g.,* plurality, *en banc,* dissent, on rehearing). Explanatory parentheticals are included in separate parentheses after the parenthesis required as part of the formal case citation.

C.   How to Cite to Authority

Cite Liberally	Heightens persuasive value of analysis. Heightens credibility.
Avoid "String Citations"	String citations are long lists of authorities standing for the same proposition.
Cite Primary Authority Whenever Possible	Cite to all relevant primary authority—statutes, regulations, cases, in that order. See Chapter I.I.3. Citations to secondary authority are discouraged in legal memoranda and briefs. If necessary to cite to secondary authority, use authority with high persuasive value. See Chapter I.E.2.
Criteria for Selection of Authority to Which to Cite	Law being applied. Jurisdiction. Court hierarchy. Similar/analogous facts. Announcement, refinement, explanation of important rules or doctrines. Year of decision—more current cases normally desirable; older landmark cases also important to cite.

D.   How to Quote from Authority

Quote Selectively	Particular relevance to issue being analyzed. Landmark cases announcing a new principle or doctrine, or modification thereto. Particularly interesting, compelling language.
Avoid Long "Block" Quotes	Block quotes are those that contain 50 words or more. Readers tend to gloss over them. If block quote is used, it should be indented on both sides, single spaced, and without quotation marks. The citation should appear outside the block quote, either before or after the quote, but in the regular text, *not* as part of the quote.

Integration of Quotes Most Desirable	Integrate short quotes with text. Language should flow uninterrupted and gramatically between text and quote(s).
Form for Quotations	Absolute precision required when quoting language from a case or other source. Use brackets ([ ]) to indicate small omissions and changes from the actual language of the quoted source. Use "..." to indicate that you are omitting language from the original quote. Never omit language in a way that is arguably misleading.

CHAPTER X

PREPARATION OF AN INTEROFFICE MEMORANDUM

A. Interoffice Memorandum[70] Generally

1. Definition of an Interoffice Memorandum

An interoffice memorandum is a document prepared by an attorney for another (usually more senior) attorney in that office.

The interoffice memorandum is intended for internal purposes and will normally be read only by the supervising attorney(s) and, perhaps, the client.

The thrust of an interoffice memorandum is to provide the reader with an analysis of the legal implications associated with a specific event or course of action (taken or proposed). The interoffice memorandum thus contains both legal and factual information.

2. Purposes of an Interoffice Memorandum

Educate and inform the reader.
Help the reader formulate and evaluate strategic options.
Help the reader counsel the client.

3. Objectivity of an Interoffice Memorandum

Given the purposes of the interoffice memorandum, it must be neutral and objective. While the writer obviously hopes that the result will favor the client's position, this must not result in a manipulation or distortion of the analysis.

The interoffice memorandum should present the full range of possibilities based on a thoughtful analysis of the law. If there are questions as

---

[70] An interoffice memorandum is often referred to as a "memo." In addition, there are other types of memoranda, such as a memoranda of law in support of or opposition to a motion (see Chapter XI.A.3.1-4.,D.) and a bench memorandum (prepared for a judge by his or her law clerk). Care should be taken not to confuse the type of memorandum at issue.

to a particular result—whether that result would be favorable to the client or not—the memorandum must present any alternative possibilities.

4. Format of an Interoffice Memorandum

The typical format for a traditional interoffice memorandum is set forth in the following pages.[71] The text of the memorandum would normally be double-spaced.

B. Guidelines for the Preparation of an Interoffice Memorandum

PRIVILEGED AND
CONFIDENTIAL/
ATTORNEY WORK
PRODUCT[72]

MEMORANDUM

TO: [Refer to your supervising attorney by his or her full, formal name.]

FROM: [Your full, formal name; initial final version.]

RE: [Give enough information to convey the client's name, and a short description of the subject matter of the memorandum. Include the case name and docket number if the matter is already in litigation.]

DATE: [Month] [day], [Year] [It is essential that you indicate the date on which you actually turn in the memorandum, so that a reader knows that both the facts and research are current through that date.]

---

[71] The form that follows is that observed by most law firms. However, firms may have their own model format, and individuals within that firm may have personal stylistic preferences. It is always best to check with your supervisor as to his or her preferred style/format.

[72] The legend "Privileged and Confidential/Attorney Work Product" does not mean that the document is privileged. Many interoffice memoranda, however, are protected from disclosure under the discovery rules. See Chapter V.C. note 56. Including such a legend on an interoffice memorandum at the very least will alert a reviewing attorney or client that the document was prepared for internal use by an attorney, and that it may be protected by the attorney-client privilege or the work-product doctrine.

Question(s) Presented

1. The Question Presented defines the legal issue which the memorandum is designed to address and answer. The Question Presented is normally framed as just that: a question. The question can be direct (beginning with "Does," or "Can," for instance) or indirect (beginning with "Whether"). If you use an indirect formulation, do not end your Question Presented with a question mark.

2. The Question Presented should usually identify the cause of action or other legal theory, the principal players, the key relevant facts, and the jurisdiction whose law will apply.

3. The Question Presented should be framed in such a way to allow the reader to readily assess what issue is addressed by and answered in the memorandum. It should be comprehensive enough and should include enough facts to give the reader a meaningful indication of what is being addressed, but it must be clear and concise enough to make it readily accessible to the reader. It should not be unduly encumbered by irrelevant facts or unnecessary verbiage. It should also be objective, and should not prejudge the outcome.

4. The Question Presented should be a single sentence, and generally should be framed so as to be *answerable* by a "yes" or "no," even if, as a substantive matter, it is not so simply answerable. It is permissible to use some other formulation if framing the question in a way that makes it answerable by a "yes" or "no" is not possible.

5. Apart from the client, who should be referred to by name or pseudonym, it is generally better to refer to other parties by their relationship to or status vis-à-vis the client rather than by their formal names. It is the relationship and/or status between the parties rather than formal names that will better define the legal issue(s) presented for resolution.

6. If your memorandum contains more than one issue, each issue should appear in a separate, numbered paragraph under the Question(s) Presented, and each issue should be addressed separately in the Legal Discussion section of the memorandum in the same order as presented in the Question(s) Presented. If your memo-

randum addresses only one issue, do not number that issue in the Question Presented section. If an issue contains sub-issues, each sub-issue may be subdivided under the primary issue stated in the Question(s) Presented. Similarly, the Legal Discussion section of your memorandum should identify and address each of these sub-issues in the same order as indicated in the Question(s) Presented section.

Brief Answer(s)

1. The Brief Answer (or Short Answer) should answer in summary form the Question Presented. It should begin with a conclusion, such as "Yes," "No," "Probably," or "Probably not." The remainder of the Brief Answer should consist of one short, self-contained paragraph (probably four sentences or fewer), which summarizes your conclusion and the reasons therefor.

2. Your Brief Answer(s) section generally should not contain citations. Exceptions to this general rule may exist in cases in which the answer depends upon a statutory provision, the issue is readily resolved by a particular case, or the reference would be to a well-established principle.

3. Many people write the Brief Answer(s) section last. If you choose to draft your Brief Answer(s) section before completing your legal analysis, be sure to return to your Brief Answer(s) before finalizing the memorandum to make sure that it accurately reflects your Legal Discussion and Conclusion.

4. You should have a separate numbered paragraph in the Brief Answer(s) section for each question presented. If your memorandum addresses only one issue, you should have a single Brief Answer, which should not be numbered. If your Question Presented has sub-parts, your Brief Answer should contain sub-parts that correspond to the structure of the Question Presented.

5. The Brief Answer(s) should normally contain little legal analysis. Present only enough detail about the outcome to enable the reader to understand the answers to the Question(s) Presented.

Statement of Facts

1. The Statement of Facts must include any and all factual information which appears in your Legal Discussion. It is a good idea to review your Statement of Facts once you have finalized the Legal Discussion and ask yourself whether you have met this requirement.

2. The Statement of Facts should include enough information to convey to a reader unfamiliar with the case a sense of what happened. If the case is already in litigation, include in the Statement of Facts the procedural history of the litigation.

3. The format of a Statement of Facts can vary, but more often than not a narrative, chronological presentation will work best. It is usually a good idea to begin the Statement of Facts with a brief recitation of who your client is and what he or she wants. Unless the case is extraordinarily complex, or has a very protracted history, the Statement of Facts should not be divided into separate sections.

4. The Statement of Facts in an interoffice memorandum must be objective, *i.e.,* the facts must be presented in a balanced fashion. In other words, do not promote your "good" facts and minimize your less favorable facts. Having said that, remember that your client may ultimately read your work product, so be careful not to be judgmental or critical of actions taken by your client. Keep to an objective account of what happened.

5. Your Statement of Facts should be just that. Do not include any analysis or argument; just the facts.

6. The Statement of Facts should be self-contained and stand on its own. Even when a document exists in real life which comprehensively sets out the facts, it is generally a good idea to create a free-standing, self-contained memorandum that can be understood without referring to or incorporating by reference other documents. You may, however, note in your Statement of Facts the source of the facts you present.

7. In the event that the information you have is in part of a subjective nature, provided to the firm by a client, for instance, it is appropriate to note the source of those facts. For instance, you may say

"According to . . ." This would be a way of dealing with unverified facts that you have no reason to doubt are true, but which may be the focus of a factual dispute among the parties.

Legal Discussion

1. The Legal Discussion section of an interoffice memorandum is where you provide the reader with your legal analysis, demonstrating the application of your facts to the relevant law.

2. The Legal Discussion will essentially embrace two elements:
   a. It will set forth the applicable body or bodies of law.
   b. It will apply the facts at hand to the applicable law.

3. Your Legal Discussion should be as "reader friendly" and accessible as possible. Treat your discussion as though the reader were not familiar with the doctrine. Leave no gaps requiring the reader to perform his or her own analysis, and make it easy for the reader to see at any given time where you are in the analysis.

4. Use of Headings:
   a. Use headings and sub-headings that correspond to the issues and sub-issues identified in your Question(s) Presented. In other words, each major point heading represented by a Roman numeral, should correspond to a Question Presented. These headings and sub-headings should be clear enough so as to allow the reader to make the transition easily from one topic to another.
   b. Headings in an interoffice memorandum are typically drafted in a neutral fashion (*e.g.,* by describing the topic under discussion in that section or sub-section), and you should be careful to ensure that they are grammatically and stylistically consistent.
   c. Headings should be *substantive* in what they communicate about the discussion that follows. In other words, they should say something about the issue to be discussed in the text that follows. Headings, for instance, should not merely indicate that a discussion of the law or of the facts of the case at hand will be discussed.

      d. Headings should be designated by a Roman numeral followed by a period, unless there is only one heading (in which case no designation is to be used). Sub-point headings are to be designated with a capital letter followed by a period. Sub-sub-point headings are to be designated with a traditional (arabic) number followed by a period.

      e. As a general matter, each major point heading should correspond to, and essentially restate, each question presented. Sub-headings within that major point heading should state the grounds or factors necessary to evaluate that question.

      f. Given the importance of headings to the overall structure of the analysis, it is a good idea to create for yourself an outline of your headings and all sub-headings. Doing so should indicate more clearly whether you have structured your headings—and hence your analysis—in a logical way. It will also enable you to see whether your headings are stylistically consistent.

5. Focus your discussion on the issue or sub-issue you are addressing; avoid long-winded academic discussions and do not get bogged down in the historical development of the doctrine at issue or in procedural or other elements of the case law that are irrelevant to your legal analysis. Your discussion should be oriented toward practical concerns and the facts and issues raised by your client's situation.

6. Keep in mind the context in which you are writing the memo. If the matter is in litigation, no doubt your focus will be different than if there is some anticipated action about which the client is concerned. Do not turn what may be the source of an action or negotiation into a discussion about how to win a case at trial.

7. The goals of an interoffice memorandum are to *educate and inform* the reader; to predict the outcome of a potential legal dispute; and to help the reader *evaluate various potential courses of action,* in part to be able to effectively *counsel the client.* Accordingly, the writer must strive to achieve balance and objectivity in the discussion. You *must* discuss cases even if they might undermine the strength of your conclusion. You *must* present the full range of possibilities, and demonstrate to the satisfaction of the reader why the outcome you predict is the most likely outcome. Ask yourself when writing an interoffice memorandum, among

other things, whether the reader has sufficient "raw materials" to reach a different conclusion, if there is, in fact, a different way of disposing of that issue. If not, your case selection and legal analysis may well be too one-sided.

8. One possible organizational approach to a typical interoffice memorandum is as follows:

    a. Discuss the law in the applicable jurisdiction:
        (1) Begin your discussion by establishing the general legal rules. Then supplement them as much as possible with relevant rules articulated in other cases.
        (2) Do not simply restate facts and holdings of relevant precedent. Develop a thematic or other framework within which to discuss these cases.
        (3) Do not at this point discuss or even allude to the facts of your case.
        (4) Do not strive to develop a treatise on the law in this area. Be pragmatic, and use cases that the reader will find relevant to the discussion of the facts at hand.
        (5) You may follow up the rule explanation with a line or two indicating what you plan to do in the discussion that follows.

    b. Apply the law to the facts of your case:
        (1) Follow up the rule explanation section with an analysis of the facts of your case under the legal framework you just established.
        (2) Divide this section into headings and subheadings to the extent appropriate to your analysis.
        (3) Begin each section with a thesis sentence to describe the issue being discussed (even though this may be redundant of the heading) and the resolution you reach of that issue.
        (4) Your analysis should focus on the facts of your case, but should call upon as may be precedent necessary to support your conclusion. Cases or detailed legal points should not be introduced in this section. References to the cases discussed in the rule explanation section should be sufficient. Some additional explanation may be necessary, especially if the legal authority was introduced much earlier in the memo.

(5) The heart of the analysis applying the law to the facts at hand will usually involve analogizing facts to and distinguishing facts from those in the applicable cases.

(6) Consistent with the goals of being objective and of educating the reader, the analysis should also point out the strengths and weaknesses of both the conclusions you reach and any considerations that tend to undermine those conclusions. This enables the reader to make certain judgments about the strength of your analysis, and about larger strategy decisions.

The best way to do this is to present your analysis of the most likely outcome, and then to present any analysis that might compel an opposite result, explaining why this outcome is not as likely as that you had predicted.[73]

(7) When a memo contains more than one issue and your resolution of the first issue suggests that the remaining issues need not be addressed (for example if a threshold requirement appears not to be met), absent instruction to the contrary from your supervisor, you should continue to analyze the remaining issues. This is because the supervisor may not agree with your analysis of the first issue, and because there is a strategic benefit in many cases to knowing how all of the relevant issues would be resolved.

(8) As a separate but related point, you will need to deal with arguably contrary authority. Depending upon the circumstances, contrary authority may be dealt with in any number of ways (see Chapter II.E.).

  • Contrary authority may not be binding on the court likely to resolve the instant dispute.
  • Contrary authority may be readily distinguishable on the facts presented.
  • Contrary authority may be inapposite because it deals with an area of law not applicable to the instant case.

---

[73] Note that this is not the same as presenting first the analysis that will most strongly support your client. Rather, it refers to the analysis that the writer thinks is most likely to prevail based on the writer's reading and analysis of the law under the facts presented.

- Contrary authority may be outdated or against the weight of authority in a majority of jurisdictions and should be overruled.[74]

(9) Each section/sub-section should end with a conclusion as to what was just addressed.

c. The entire body of law applicable to the question presented need not be addressed all at the same time. The body of law applicable to a particular issue may be followed by the analysis of the facts as they apply to that legal issue. Then, the memo may continue to set forth the law applicable to the next legal issue, followed by the analysis of the facts in connection with that issue.

It must be remembered that if a body of law is applicable to more than one issue, it must be presented in advance of the application of that law to the relevant set of facts.

9. If you think more facts would be necessary in order to reach a definitive conclusion or complete your legal analysis, say so and why.

10. You will undoubtedly notice that, in certain circumstances, there will be a large number of cases in your jurisdiction relevant to your issue. The use of string citations (a list of cases standing for a cited proposition) is generally discouraged, so the question arises: how does a lawyer select which cases to use in a memorandum? This is not an easy question to answer, nor is it an easy task to master. Over time you will develop a sense for which cases to use and which to omit, but there are some general rules that can be applied:

a. Focus on cases that are more factually analogous to the case at hand. Remember that "factually analogous" is not "factually identical." Allow yourself to be flexible enough to see factual similarities where they might not be immediately apparent.

b. Use other cases, even if factually distinct, to the extent that they seem to explain or modify important rules or doctrines addressed in earlier cases, or to the extent that they may be considered to be landmark cases in the jurisprudence on your issue.

---

[74] Higher level courts are more empowered to overrule applicable precedent than are lower courts. See Chapter I.F.7.

   c.   Remember the hierarchy of courts within your jurisdiction. Obviously, it is preferable to include more cases from higher courts than from lower courts, but lower court cases may at times be extremely important, and you should not shy away from using them. Court level is only one factor to be considered in selecting cases.

   d.   Similarly, all other things being equal, it is preferable to rely upon more recent cases than upon older cases. Of course, all other things are rarely, if ever, equal. You may find cases that have become landmarks in that they continue to be cited and relied upon frequently. There may also be old cases that are more factually relevant than newer cases and which you would not want to ignore in your legal analysis. Accordingly, do not discard old cases for that reason alone. A good way to show the court that a rather old case remains good law is to indicate that it has been cited or quoted with approval in a newer case.

   e.   In the absence of relevant authority in your jurisdiction, it is appropriate to cite to opinions issued by other state courts or to federal court decisions which apply your state or some other state's law.

11.   All citations to authority belong in the text of the memo. Footnotes should be used sparingly, generally to raise points of interest to the issue discussed but that are not directly relevant to the issue under analysis. Footnotes may also be used for potentially relevant areas of analysis that you consider to be beyond the ambit of your assignment.

12.   Remember to use proper citation form as outlined in the *Bluebook*. You will recall that introductory signals and parentheticals are used with great frequency in legal documents. You should try to use introductory signals (see *Bluebook* Rules 1.2 and 1.3) and parentheticals (see *Bluebook* Rule 1.5) as often as possible. As indicated in Rule 1.5, parentheticals are very often employed in conjunction with introductory signals. See Chapter IX.

Conclusion

1. Your Conclusion should summarize your legal analysis. This should be in a somewhat greater level of detail than appears in the Brief Answer, and should provide a more thorough description of the reasons supporting the ultimate conclusions reached in your memorandum.

2. The Conclusion should also provide the reader with any practical suggestions or recommendations that you might have based on your research and analysis. In addition, you can mention additional issues that should be researched or otherwise addressed, but which you understand to be beyond the scope of your task.

3. Although there may be degrees of certainty with which you can predict the outcome as to each particular issue, your Conclusion should be as definitive as possible, without misleading the reader, misrepresenting the state of the law, or ignoring the risks. Remember that the purpose of your memorandum is to inform the reader as to the legal issue presented so that the reader can advise the client how to proceed. A Conclusion that states nothing more than "I don't know" will not have served that purpose.

4. The Conclusion should not be divided into separate sections to correspond to the various issues, nor generally should it contain citations.

CHAPTER XI

PREPARATION OF A MOTION AND MEMORANDUM OF LAW IN SUPPORT OF OR OPPOSITION THERETO

A. Motions Generally

1. Definition of a Motion

A motion is an affirmative request for relief from a court.

Motions may be filed seeking virtually any type of order from the court, relating to topics ranging from the mundane to the controversial.

2. Parties to Motion Practice

Any party may file a motion.

Regardless of the posture of that party with respect to the litigation, the party filing the motion is called the "movant."

The party answering or responding to the motion is the "respondent."

3. Definition of a Memorandum in Support of or Opposition to a Motion

Provides the legal analysis that justifies the grounds for granting or opposing the motion, respectively.

4. Purposes of a Memorandum in Support of or Opposition to a Motion

Educate and inform the court.

Show strong hand in the hopes of exacting favorable settlement concessions from opponent.

Other strategic possibilities, such as concealing certain information or strategies.

5. General Format for Motions

A motion is generally filed as a separate document, and focuses on the nature of the relief sought by the moving party. The motion itself will be short, and will describe the parties, the relief sought, and a general statement of the legal basis upon which the motion is premised.

A document referred to as a memorandum of points and authorities in support of the motion is generally filed along with the motion. As its name suggests, that document sets forth in detail the factual and legal bases for the relief sought in the motion. This is what many practitioners often refer to as the "brief."[75]

Also generally attached to a motion is a draft order, which the movant proposes be entered by the court. The proposed order is generally complete, except for the signature of the judge and the date entered.

Applicable court rules should always be consulted; this format may not be appropriate in all courts or for all types of motions, and court rules will generally establish more specific requirements for the filing of motions.

6. Time for Filing Motions

Court rules may prescribe time periods appropriate to the filing of particular types of motions.

Some motions may be filed at any time; other motions must be filed within a specified period of time as may be required by court rule or order.

B. Draft Motion

As indicated above (see Chapter XI.A.), a motion is a request by a party to the court for some specified relief. What follows is a prototype for a traditional motion.

As always, it is critical to consult local rules to ensure that they are followed.

---

[75] Reference to the Memorandum of Law in motion practice as a "brief" is something of a misnomer. The term "briefs" is traditionally reserved for trial and appellate briefs, not memoranda of law in support of or opposition to a motion.

[Complete case caption, including court and case number.]

MOTION

[May instead be entitled "[party designation] Motion For An Order Granting [state nature of the relief specified below."]

[Party designation][party name] hereby moves this court for an order [state nature of the relief sought].

The grounds for this motion are set forth in the accompanying memorandum of points and authorities.

DATED: [city], [state] [date submitted]

Respectfully submitted,

_____

[Counsel's name]
[Law firm name and address]
Attorneys for [party destination]
[Party name]

C. Draft Order

Normally, a party filing a motion is required to submit a Draft Order with the motion. The Draft Order sets forth the relief sought in the motion. The court will sometimes use the Draft Order to order the relief requested, or the court may draft its own order.

Local rule may also require that the party opposing the motion file a Draft Order with which the court may deny the motion.

The following is a Draft Order that would accompany a motion.

[Complete case caption, including court and case number.]

ORDER

Upon consideration of the motion of [party filing motion] for [nature of relief sought] and the opposition thereto, this Court hereby ORDERS that the motion be granted and [describe the relief sought].

ENTERED this _____ day of _____ , 19 __ .

_____

[Name of Judge]
[Title, *e.g.,* United States District Court Judge]

D. Guidelines for the Preparation of a Memorandum of Law in Support of or Opposition to a Motion

As indicated above (see Chapter XI.A.), the memorandum in support of or opposition to a motion sets forth the legal analysis in support of or in opposition to the motion.

The following prototype is based on a memorandum of law in opposition to a motion for summary judgment. Apart from those points placed in brackets, which are specific to summary judgment, the remainder of the opposition is applicable generally to motion practice.

Local rules should always be consulted for variations from court to court.

[Complete case caption, including court and case number.]

PLAINTIFF'S MEMORANDUM OF LAW
IN OPPOSITION TO DEFENDANT'S
MOTION FOR [SUMMARY JUDGMENT]

1. In one short, self-contained paragraph, identify the parties (giving, within parentheses and in quotations, the shortened name you will use in the document to refer to each party), the nature of the lawsuit, perhaps a *few* details about the case, the procedural posture, and the position your client is taking on the motion before the court [*e.g.,* opposition to motion for summary judgment].[76]

2. A chronological approach to the preliminary statement generally works best.

3. The preliminary statement must be short and concise. It should be a single paragraph, probably containing no more than two or three sentences. Its sole function is to help orient the court as to the nature of the pleading and the procedural context in which it was filed.

4. The preliminary statement will be rather bland, short, and focused closely on procedural matters. Nevertheless, you should take this opportunity to begin to develop the reader's sympathy for your position.

5. There should be no heading for this section; it should simply begin immediately following the caption and title of the pleading. See note 76.

---

[76] This portion of the memorandum of law is often referred to as the "Preliminary Statement," although no such heading precedes it. It simply appears after the name of the document listed in the caption.

STATEMENT OF FACTS

1. The Statement of Facts should contain all of the factual information necessary to support your legal argument. You may not in your Argument rely upon or refer to facts that were not presented in the Statement of Facts.

2. In addition to its comprehensive nature, the Statement of Facts is intended to be persuasive. This is the first real opportunity you have to persuade the reader of the propriety of the relief you are seeking. *Be an advocate.* Frame the facts in the way most favorable to your client.

3. Having said that, be certain that every word in your Statement of Facts is beyond reproach. Do not be misleading. Do not distort the facts. Do not omit material facts that are necessary to present a complete picture of what happened. Indeed, the Statement of Facts is the perfect place to confront what I call "unfortunate facts" in a non-argumentative way: present unfortunate facts and neutralize them as much as possible by juxtaposing them with favorable facts.

4. A good Statement of Facts is not a dry recitation of facts but a story, punctuated with color. Do not simply summarize the testimony by dryly relating the testimony of various witnesses. Instead, interweave the testimony from various witnesses to shape the narrative and make your story compelling. Lead the reader toward your conclusion and imbue your Statement of Facts with a strong sense of the theory of your case. Upon reading the Statement of Facts, the judge should be ready to rule in your favor. Use this as a test for editing your work.

5. Limit yourself to the facts, but use transitional words and phrases to shape the narrative and move the story along.

6. Do not be argumentative or appear to make conclusions in the Statement of Facts, but use artful word choices to set the right tone and suggest obvious inferences. Conversely, use more neutral language to diminish the impact of unfavorable facts.

7. When referring to the testimony of your witnesses, words like "testified," "indicated," "noted," "observed," "confirmed," and "emphasized," to name a few, make good choices. When referring to the testimony of adverse witnesses, words like "suggested" and "contended" are good choices; when trying to undermine that testimony, words like "acknowledged," "admitted," and "conceded" make good choices. But avoid *ad hominem* attacks on witnesses and on your opponents.

8. Identify each witness the first time you refer to him/her by stating his/her full name ("Mr." and "Ms." are unnecessary) and title or position. Use only the person's last name when referring to him/her subsequently.

9. Generally, a chronological approach to the Statement of Facts works best. Your Statement of Facts can end with a brief description of procedural history, but this should only include the filing of the lawsuit (including, perhaps, reference to the damages sought by the plaintiff). You need not repeat the procedural posture of the motion indicated in the preliminary statement.

10. Include citations to the record (that is, the compilation of factual information involved in the case) for every factual allegation made in the Statement of Facts (and, for that matter, in the Argument). See also the *Bluebook* at P.7. It is acceptable to use *"id."* to refer to the immediately preceding record citation, if the prior citation contains only that reference. It is a good idea to *not* use *"id."* at all until you are nearing a final draft. If you end up making changes in drafting, having a lot of *"ids."* around can make editing more difficult and you risk confusing your references. Record citations should appear often in your Statement of Facts. Do not make the reader guess the source of your information. It is imperative that you make it easy for the judge or clerk to find the place in the record where a fact to which you are citing can be found.

11. [In writing a memorandum of law in favor of or opposition to a motion for summary judgment, you will want to cite to facts from documents *other than* the pleadings in the case, unless the fact is truly uncontroverted. Remember that a pleading (Complaint, Answer and Counterclaim, Motion for Summary Judgment, etc.) reflects the allegations of the party filing the pleading, and nothing more. Deposition testimony and responses to other forms of discovery are very effective sources of factual information to demonstrate the existence of a genuine issue of material fact. Remember that what you may think is a logical explanation for something, but which lacks a foundation in the record, does not raise a "genuine" issue of fact adequate to survive a motion for summary judgment.]

12. It is acceptable to use quotes from the record in the Statement of Facts. Be sure that your use of quotations from the record does not detract from the narrative, flowing nature of your Statement of Facts. Try to integrate them with your own text.

ARGUMENT

1. The Argument must start with a major point heading, which is a one-sentence statement of your Argument. There may be more than one major point heading, which will correspond to the number of legal issues. Each major heading will be preceded by a roman numeral followed by a period. The heading itself will be in all capital letters.

2. Sub-headings should be more specific and reflect sub-issues presented under each major point heading. Sub-headings should be preceded by a capital letter followed by a period, and underlined. Use upper and lower case letters for

the text of the sub-headings (capitalize the first letter of *each* word), and follow them with a period. Sub-headings, like major point headings, should state an affirmative proposition which you will prove in that section of the Argument.

3.   Taken together, the major point headings and sub-headings should describe the grounds for your argument. Each major point should reflect a complete and independent basis for a ruling in your client's favor. Each sub-point should support that main heading. Headings (major and subsidiary) should not only state the proposition but should contain, concisely, enough facts and law to indicate why your thesis is correct.

4.   All headings (including sub-headings) are to be underlined, end with a period, and should be single-spaced when longer than one line.

5.   A useful test for whether your headings are framed properly is: Are they specific enough to preclude their application in another case, but for the names of the parties?

6.   After the major point heading but before the sub-headings, it may be appropriate to include some of the substance of your argument. For instance, if portions of your argument go to the entire issue presented by that major point heading, include it before you get to the sub-headings.

7.   If the same legal issue applies to more than one major point heading, the appropriate place to set forth the general parameters of that issue may be before *any* of the major point headings. The main goal in this respect is to state the law or an issue in a place where, as a matter of logic and organization, it will be seen as applicable to those sections that follow it.

8.   Most motions involve areas of law that are somewhat familiar to the court. Accordingly, it is best not to overdo a discussion of the law that the judge is likely to already know. The resolution of most motions is likely to be fact-specific, so placing particular emphasis on the facts is usually a much better expenditure of the writer's time and space.

9.   Different instructors of legal writing advocate slightly different formulations for writing a legal analysis. Without resorting to formulaic constructions, the following elements are critical in preparing an analysis for a memorandum of law in support of or opposition to a motion:
   a.   The major point heading should represent the issue presented.
   b.   A thesis sentence/paragraph (short) should follow the major point heading and essentially restate the major point heading. That is, it should present the issue to be addressed and the writer's perspective on the issue.
   c.   A discussion of the *reason* why the court should come out the way you have suggested. This will include a discussion of the law relating to the issue presented.

     d. An analysis of the law presented in light of the facts of your case. This may require division into sub-headings so that the reader can clearly see the analysis for each of the points that, taken together, show why you prevail on the merits. This discussion will also include a discussion of why any seemingly contrary authority does not control the outcome here. See Chapter II.G.
        Each sub-section will follow the general organization described above, and will end with a conclusion as to that particular point.

     e. Each section will end with a conclusion restating what you have just shown.

10. Recall that the Argument will be very fact-centered and may contain very little legal discussion or analysis. It is essential, however, that you make explicit the connection between the law and the facts.

11. In addition, use record citations for every fact to which you refer or upon which you rely in your Argument. You will probably want to repeat facts for the reader that appeared in the Statement of Facts as you rely on them in the Argument, especially the favorable ones. And even though you need to mention facts in the Statement of Facts to which you will refer in the Argument, you can discuss the facts here in greater detail or use more extensive and/or different quotes in making your legal argument.

12. Recall that the non-moving party opposing most motions is not trying to win the case on the merits. Thus, be vigilant about framing your conclusions and propositions in the proper procedural context. [A conclusion appropriate to the summary judgment context would be "Therefore, a reasonable jury could find that" or "There is ample evidence to suggest that" or "There is a genuine issue of material fact as to whether . . . ."]

13. [There are at least two effective ways to establish the existence of doubt as to factual matters in opposing a motion for summary judgment:

     a. Affirmatively highlight facts that support your client's view of the facts and which differ from your adversary's explanation of those same events.

     b. Cast doubt upon the testimony of your opponent's witnesses and facts by attacking their credibility or otherwise undermining their testimony.]

CONCLUSION

Different attorneys take different approaches to the Conclusion. Some attorneys like to use the Conclusion to summarize the substance of the argument just presented. Another approach (which this author prefers) is to simply state "For the foregoing reasons" *or* "Accordingly" ["party on whose behalf the brief is filed] respectively requests that the Court [provide the requested relief]." If you need to elaborate, chances are your legal argument is not clear or cogent enough.

DATED: City, State [date submitted]

Respectfully submitted,

_____

[Your name, firm name and address]
Attorney for [name of party]

CHAPTER XII

PREPARATION OF AN APPELLATE BRIEF

A. Appellate Briefs Generally

1. Appellate Courts Review Lower Tribunals for Errors of Law

As discussed above (see Chapter VI.A.), the appellate process is limited to issues of law. Unless the lower tribunal (trial court or agency) made an egregious error with respect to some factual issue, the court of appeals will accept the factual determinations of the tribunal below and review the lower tribunal's determinations only for errors of law.

2. The Appellate Practitioner Should Limit the Brief to Alleged Errors of Law

Accordingly, the practitioner should limit his or her arguments on appeal to legal issues, *i.e.,* issues of the type that an appellate court is likely to entertain.

In addition, the practitioner should tailor the brief to highlight the legal errors, generally assuming *arguendo* that the facts as found by the lower tribunal are true.

3. The Process for Filing Appellate Briefs

The "opening brief" is filed by the appellant or petitioner (see Chapter VI.B.), within the time prescribed by court rule or order.

A "responsive brief" is filed by the appellee or respondent (see Chapter VI.B.), within a prescribed time period after the submission of the opening brief.

The appellant or petitioner will then file a "reply brief" within a specified time after submission of the responsive brief. The reply brief is to be limited to the arguments raised in the responsive brief.

4. Importance of Following All Applicable Rules and Practices

The Federal Rules of Appellate Procedure establish a uniform set of rules for appellate practice before the federal courts. In addition, each circuit court has its own set of local rules which must be followed before that circuit. Each circuit also has its own set of operating rules, which should be consulted.

State appeals courts also have rules of procedure which must be consulted and followed.

B. Guidelines for the Preparation of an Appellate Brief

As indicated above (see Chapter VI.A.2.), an appeal may be taken from a district court determination or from a final agency action.

As noted (see Chapters IV.B. and XII.A.4.), local court rules and procedures may provide additional specific rules for the filing of briefs. Such rules will modify the model set forth below, and hence should always be consulted and adhered to.

The following prototype is a brief of appellant in a federal circuit court, based on Rule 28 of the Federal Rules of Appellate Procedure.

IN THE UNITED STATES COURT OF APPEALS FOR THE
[NUMBER/NAME OF CIRCUIT] CIRCUIT

[Full case heading]

BRIEF OF APPELLANT [NAME OF PARTY]

TABLE OF CONTENTS

1. Table of Contents should reflect all parts of the brief, with page numbers.

2. Be certain to check your final pagination to ensure that the Table of Contents accurately reflects any last-minute changes to the brief itself.

TABLE OF CASES AND AUTHORITIES

1. List of cases and other authorities cited in the brief.

2. Cases are to be listed first, in alphabetical order.

3. Other authorities should be listed after cases—constitutional provisions, statutes, regulatory sources, legislative history, secondary authorities, and other authorities, in that order.

4. Add page numbers to reflect location in brief where each reference can be found. Use *passim* for references to authorities that appear often.

STATEMENT OF SUBJECT MATTER AND APPELLATE JURIDICTION

1. Statement, supported by applicable citations, of the basis for jurisdiction in the district court or agency from which the appeal arose.

2. Statement, supported by applicable citations, of the basis for jurisdiction in the court of appeals. This statement must include relevant dates so as to show the timeliness of appellate review.[77]

ISSUES PRESENTED FOR REVIEW

1. The statement of issues in the appeal brief should be presented in adversarial form.

2. Present the issues in a way that suggests the answer. One test to help determine whether the issues are framed in a way that adequately presents them in an adversarial format is to consider whether a judge reading the issues presented for review would be persuaded that the lower court or agency decision should be reversed.

STATEMENT OF THE CASE

1. The Statement of the Case may be thought of as the procedural history of the case.

2. The Statement of the Case is to indicate briefly the nature of the case and the course of the proceedings below, including the disposition of the court or agency below.

3. The Statement of the Case should also include a statement of the facts relevant to the appeal. As in the Statement of Facts for a motion (see Chapter XI. B.), the Statement of Facts in an appellate brief should set out the facts in a fair and honest way, but should be presented in a way that tells the story in the most advantageous way to the position you are advocating in your brief. Punctuate the facts with appropriate (but not excessive) adjectives, and juxtapose events so as to make the facts sympathetic to your position.

---

[77] The time for filing a notice of appeal or a petition for review (see Chapter VI.5.) is often prescribed by statute. When the statutory time limit has expired, depending upon the language of the statute, the court may be without authority to hear the appeal.

4. Citations to facts in the Statement of Facts (and throughout the brief) should be to the Record. See Chapter VI.B. The relevant portions of the record are to be reproduced for the court and submitted with the brief. In the alternative, the parties may file a "Deferred Appendix" after the submission of all briefs, along with new briefs with record citations to the Deferred Appendix. See Rule 30(c) of the Federal Rules of Appellate Procedure.

SUMMARY OF ARGUMENT

1. A good summary is not merely a recitation of the Argument, but should encapsulate the main theories of the Argument into a concise story that, on its own, suggests the reasons for the relief sought. Again, ask yourself whether the judges would be persuaded of your position simply on the basis of the Summary of the Argument.

ARGUMENT

1. The Argument should be framed such that each part of the Argument matches one of the Issues Presented for Review, and in the same order. As with motion practice (see Chapter XI.D.), the Argument should present a persuasive legal analysis of the grounds for the relief sought.

2. The Argument should contain references to the Record.

CONCLUSION

1. The Conclusion should be brief.

2. The Conclusion should state the explicit relief sought, noting support for that result "For the foregoing reasons."

DATED: City, State [date submitted]

Respectfully submitted,

_____

[Your name, firm name and address]
Attorney for Appellant [name of party]

INDEX